# PREACHING ON
# NATIONAL
# HOLIDAYS

# PREACHING ON NATIONAL HOLIDAYS

edited by

Alton M. Motter

FORTRESS PRESS     Philadelphia

Library of Congress Catalog Card Number 75–36–445

ISBN 0–8006–1222–1

5400K75     Printed in U.S.A.     1–1222

# CONTENTS

# FOREWORD

The observance of our national holidays is evidence of the way the religious values of the Judeo-Christian faith and American civil religion are intertwined.

Holidays are more than mere holidays. They are a part of our national "ceremonial calendar," to quote a phrase used by Will Herberg. As such, they form a symbol system of America's civil religion, which he has described as the "religionization of the national life and national culture."* And most of these holidays are recognized or observed in many of our churches and synagogues in one way or another.

For some time we have been hearing a great deal about the place of "civil religion" in American life. Robert N. Bellah did much to illumine the subject in an article under that title which appeared in the Winter 1967 issue of *Daedalus*, the journal of the American Academy of Arts and Sciences.† Since then thoughtful writers have dealt with the responsibility of church and synagogue leaders to help determine the future shape of civil religion in America.

The contributors to this anthology are sharing in that process. They represent many religious backgrounds. In addition to nine Protestant denominations, including Quaker, Mennonite, and Evangelical Free Church, there are also sermons from distinguished Roman Catholic and Jewish leaders. Four of these are parish pastors, four are bishops and denominational heads, six are college and seminary professors, four are ecumenical leaders; one is a United States senator, one a congressman, and one an evangelist. The writers come from every major section of America.

* See Will Herberg, "America's Civil Religion: What It Is and Whence It Comes," *Modern Age Quarterly* (Summer 1973).
† Reprinted in *American Civil Religion*, ed. Russell E. Richey and Donald G. Jones (New York: Harper and Row, 1974).

The Thanksgiving sermon by Archbishop Joseph L. Bernardin deals with the theme of civil religion in the most direct fashion. But all the sermons are either directly or indirectly related to it. The reader will find solid nourishment here for enhancing the spiritual life. There is also much helpful guidance for a higher quality of national and world citizenship.

ALTON M. MOTTER

# THE NEW YEAR: A TIME GIVEN BY GOD

*Robert V. Moss*

*President, United Church of Christ,*
*New York, New York*

The ways in which we Americans celebrate the beginning of the new year are diverse and colorful. Hundreds of thousands of us gather in Times Square in New York City to watch as an illuminated ball on top of the Allied Chemical Tower falls at the precise moment the new year begins. Millions more are watching on television. In many communities church bells still ring out the old and in the new. The bells more often than not are echoed by firecrackers and other fireworks despite city and state ordinances. Local congregations of Christians come together for "watch night" services to keep serious vigil as the old year wanes and the new waxes. In public places and at family hearths people join in singing "Auld Lang Syne" as a salute to the good old times, lift "a cup of kindness," and embrace one another affectionately. It is a time of nostalgia—looking back at the old year. It is a time of hope—symbolizing a new beginning. It is a time of self-examination and new commitment—hence New Year's resolutions.

Let us reflect briefly on these aspects of the New Year's celebration in the light of Christian tradition. To do so fruitfully, however, requires that we consider for a moment the way in which time is understood and measured in the biblical tradition.

While we may measure time quantitatively in terms of hours and days and months and years, it is more characteristic of biblical writers to measure time qualitatively—in terms of what happens rather than in terms of duration. Consequently they are more likely to talk about "the year that King Uzziah died" than to define that year in terms of the number of years since the establishment of the kingdom or even the Exodus. Or again, they will speak of "seedtime" and "harvesttime" or "the time that she should be delivered."

1

In these phrases we can begin to see that from the biblical point of view time is seen as an opportunity given by God to which we are called to respond. At seedtime we must respond by sowing. At harvesttime the appropriate response is to reap. We then are called upon to discern the times—to seek to discover what God is calling us to be and to do at this particular time which is given us. Usually the biblical writers use the term *chronos*, from which comes our word "chronological," when they want to speak of quantitative time, *kairos* when they would speak of qualitative time.

For Christians, therefore, it is not enough to say that the new year marks the beginning of another measurement of time—that in 365 days the New Year's babe will become a bearded figure who will disappear as another baby takes its place. Rather we are called to ask ourselves and one another as a new year begins, What opportunity or opportunities is God giving us to which we must respond? It is easy to answer the question, What is the *chronos?* It is 1977 or 1978. It is not so easy to answer the question, What is the *kairos?* But we are at least reminded that this is the question we need to answer when we speak of the new year as A.D. 1977, or A.D. 1978. This is *anno domini*, the year of our Lord. And it is to Jesus Christ's lordship over this year, over us, and over the world to which we are called to bear witness.

It was suggested earlier that the celebration of New Year's Day is a time (a *kairos*) of looking back. The danger is that we look back in an unbiblical way. There is a lot of nostalgia in American culture today. And like neuralgia it is a kind of sickness—because it is a form of escapism. Martin Marty reminds us that in the nostalgic productions of Hollywood and Broadway we seem to be able to remember the thirties without the depression, the forties without the war, and the fifties without McCarthyism. Or as a line from the lyrics of the theme song of the film, *The Way We Were*, puts it: "What's too painful to remember we simply choose to forget."

The biblical writers do not recall their past in this way. When Paul writes about the Exodus, he writes about it "warts and all." He reminds the Corinthians that many were faithless and were destroyed, even though the Exodus was the event which brought the people of God into being (1 Cor. 10: 1–11).

What then is the purpose of recalling the past? Christians look realistically at the past in order to use it as a resource for the present and the future. This is the biblical understanding of the use of the past. Before the children of Israel entered into Canaan, Joshua called them together and told their story, beginning with Abraham in Ur of the Chaldees to that very moment when they were gathered there. And he concluded with the challenge: "And if you be unwilling to serve the Lord, choose this day whom you will serve...; but as for me and my house, we will serve the Lord" (Josh. 24:15).

New Year's is an appropriate time, then, for looking at the past year and the years before that. But let us look at it realistically with the purpose of making better choices in the year ahead.

The new year is a time of hope, also. But what kind of hope? And hope based on what? Mary Martin sings in *South Pacific*: "I'm stuck like a dope with a thing called hope...." And that may be the case with many of us. New Year's gives us an opportunity to reexamine our hopes in the light of the Christian faith. For some, the hope of their lives has been that nebulous thing called "the American Dream." Unfortunately that Dream has become so materialistic and individualistic—so selfish—that it has led to disillusionment for many who have "attained it" and despair for those who have not.

The hope of which the biblical tradition speaks is a "new and living hope" which is both personal and corporate. It is the hope that each person will come "to maturity, to the measure of the stature of the fullness of Christ" (Eph. 4:13) and that all shall dwell together in a "city which has foundations, whose builder and maker is God" (Heb. 11:10). That is the hope by which Christians should judge all human and political promises for a better day and a better world, whether cast in terms of a new deal, a great society, or a new world. For us the hope is for justice, liberation, and human fulfillment in this world and an unbroken life with God in the world to come.

On what is this hope based? It is based on God's power revealed in the Resurrection of Jesus Christ. Not even death can ultimately frustrate God, who is at work making all things new. And our hope is based on what we see God doing now, judging people and nations according to righteousness and saving us from aimlessness and sin. Therefore our hope for the new year cannot be selfish; it is the hope that the deeper longings of humankind will be in greater measure fulfilled according to the promises of God.

Finally, the new year provides an opportunity for self-examination and new commitment. As a consequence of our tragic experience in Vietnam, most Americans know that Tet is the time of the celebration of the new year for the Vietnamese. It is basically a family time. And in the course of the celebration the family gathers for a time of reflection. The head of the family, the father, during this period addresses each member of the family—his wife and each of the children. He points out to each of them the ways in which they have grown during the year which is closing. He also points out where there are weaknesses and the need for further growth. Each member of the family promises to strive to conquer any weakness.

Our practice of making resolutions at New Year's is not unlike the Vietnamese practice. But there is a sense in which self-examination is inadequate. We ought to look at ourselves through the eyes of others whom we trust and who know us and who can speak the truth in love. And we ought not to flinch from making our resolutions known to the community in which we find strength. Speaking in terms of the Christian tradition, this is what is meant by the mutual ministry of believers. God gives us an opportunity to make new and deeper commitments as the new year begins. And we can sing with Tennyson:

> Ring out the feud of rich and poor,
> Ring in redress to all mankind.
> .    .    .    .    .
>
> Ring out false pride in place and blood,
> The civic slander and the spite;
> Ring in the love of truth and right,
> Ring in the common love of good.
> *(In Memoriam A. H. H.*
> 106.11,12,21–24)

# BETWEEN THE ALREADY AND THE NOT YET

*Ralph W. Loew*

*Pastor Emeritus, Holy Trinity Lutheran Church, Buffalo,
New York; Director, Department of Religion,
Chautauqua Institution, Chautauqua, New York*

In the beginning was the Word, and the Word was with God, and
the Word was God. He was in the beginning with God; all things
were made through him, and without him was not anything made
that was made. In him was life and the life was the light of men.
The light shines in the darkness, and the darkness has not overcome it.
There was a man sent from God whose name was John. He came
for testimony, to bear witness to the light, that all might believe
through him. He was not the light, but came to bear witness to the
light.                                                         John 1:1–8

A sermon for New Year's Day? One doesn't think of this day in
terms of sermons and liturgical worship. Yet the ancient calendars carried the notation that this was the Feast of the Circumci-
sion. It was a time to note that the obedient Jewish couple took
the baby Jesus to the synagogue to observe an ancient Mosaic
law. So there it is—a day which ranged from pagan rites to
religious worship. Whatever the significance of the day in our
own time, it remains as a symbol of a universal need to deal with
time and our own understanding of the presence of God in that
time.

A series of scientific experiments concerning time are going on
in various parts of the world just now. Willing volunteers have
permitted themselves to be entombed in underground caves for
periods of months. They have food and water. They are isolated, cut off from all normal communication and routines. Scien-
tists want to determine how a human being reacts in such situations. What happens to our normal time patterns of sleeping and
eating? What is New Year's Day in such a situation?

If that is difficult to imagine, then look again at the revolutionary changes that are occurring in society. The erosion of estab-

5

lished values seems an almost parallel situation to the darkened cave. Long ago Plato told a myth of the cave and the chained prisoners whose knowledge consisted only of what they could learn from the flickering shadows on the wall before them. Then he revealed their astonishment upon being permitted to see the full source of light.

It is this light in the cave of existence which John notes. "In the beginning was the Word and the Word was with God and the Word was God. He was in the beginning with God; all things were made by him and without him was not anything made that was made. In him was the life and the life was the light of men. The light shines in the darkness, and the darkness has not overcome it." There is more than poetic symbolism here. It is the understanding that between that which has already happened and that which is not yet, there is a reality which must be dealt with in every age.

Time then is not just turning the page of the calendar, trying to get accustomed to writing a new date on our checks and going about the artificial markings of time. There is a Presence, which was at the heart of the universe in its beginnings and which reaches into futures as mysterious as the mysteries of that universe.

In the midst of that mystery, there is the mystery of ourselves. There, says John, is the record of God's presence. Not just as an idea or a distant legend or tale. It is in our own flesh, in our own experience and in our own calendars that this experience has been known. The name of Emmanuel—God with us—has been known in the presence of a life like our life. To see that, for the first time or the thousandth, is to have a New Year's Day! This, then, is the basis of the Christian hope, that God is with us, that nothing is able to separate us from the love of God in Christ Jesus.

On the sharp edge of a dividing line of time, Christians look Janus-like in both directions. The Christian witness deals with reality and with the present, but it does this in the perspective of what has already happened and what is yet to be. Between the Creation and the Incarnation to the faith in a God whose care is continuing, we stand at New Year's Day. "We have known this light and the darkness cannot put it out."

That fact changes a point of view. The world was the same the day after Galileo revealed his new understanding of the universe, but the point of view was different. The world was the same the day after Columbus discovered America, but the point of view was different. The world before the astronauts walked on the moon was the same as it was the day after their giant step, yet men looking down upon the incredible beauty of their planet had a new point of view. These ecstasies in the eternal world are evidences of an inner world experience. Without him was not anything made that was made. He became flesh and dwelt among us. There is a light which no darkness can put out. Happy New Year!

Caught between a towering past—nothing was made without him—and an equally towering future—the darkness cannot put out the light—John literally sings his faith. We need to follow his example. On one occasion Harry Emerson Fosdick said in his own inimitable way: "We defend religion too much. Religion like good music needs no defense but rendition. A wrangling controversy in defense of religion is precisely as if every member of the orchestra would beat folks on the head with their violins to prove that music is beautiful. Such procedure is no way to prove it."

Yet we try that procedure with debates ranging from the ordination of women to the authenticity of Scripture until the world about us only hears the discords instead of the harmony. Much more comes from the exciting dialogues that go on in our time between Roman Catholics and Jews, or between Lutherans and Roman Catholics. Such conversations come as a kind of new epiphany bringing new searchers for truth following a star.

Dialogues don't cancel the past, but they do usher in a new year. They represent the very tension of our hope. They recognize the unfulfilled dream, the need to draw a line across time itself and usher in a new year of possibilities. Grace and hope are always held in such tension. He who came, full of grace and truth, becoming flesh in our existence, can move us out of our helpless contentment with joyless, negative damnations which keep mankind from the newness of any year.

Just now there is so much despair, such hopelessness, and such agony of body and spirit that all creation cries out for a newness. How can the Word become flesh among the starving in Sahelian Africa, or reality for the despairing refugees in so many parts of the world, or a reconciling presence for the growing polarizations between races and groups in our own country? Studs Terkel, who interviewed numbers of persons at their daily work, concluded that too many of us are trapped in the syndrome of helplessness. He called it "the hired hand" helplessness, where there is no one to take personal responsibility or to move toward any sense of moral power. Think of it. In this day when people so often seem to deny the centuries of civilizing culture, there is this record in John of a transaction of grace. God, who made all that is made, is among us. In the whole of life!

My own beloved grandfather, who lived in our household when I was a boy, spoke a fluent English even though his native tongue was German. When he came home in the evening he insisted on speaking German. We who were the children of the household would protest saying, "Speak English, Grandpa." "Nein, Kinder," he would state firmly, "English is to make money with, German is to pray with." Don't laugh too long. Too many of us have tried across our personal history to draw that neat line between our words of faith and our deeds, encasing religion within neat boundaries. "Nothing was made without him." When that sinks in, there is a New Year of grace, an awareness of God's presence in the whole of life. We are delivered from that horror of making others "nonpersons," which is what Erich Fromm says every tyrant has done. Hitler did that with the Jews, we did it when we called the Vietnamese "gooks," we tried it at Attica, and we are tempted to do it whenever we are content with that old way. Yet the word is clear: "Without him was not anything made," and the mind rushes off to that grace-filled New Year when there is neither Jew nor Greek, male nor female.

Elia Kazan, in his novel, *The Arrangement*, tells of a poignant dealing of a son with his father. The old man was always cantankerous and now he was dying. His mind was wandering. Eddie was standing at the bedside watching his father. "He wanted to talk with an old friend in Turkey. He wanted out of the hospital. He wanted to see Anatolia. Then," says Eddie, "I had it, the sensation. For the first time in my life I looked at him, crazed as he was, not as a problem to be dealt with, not as authority to handle and evade, but as a human whose being was opened and revealed to me so that I could see that his troubles were like my troubles. He was one human and I was another. He was my brother." The tragedy is that all too often we come to the miracle of that revealing moment only when the year is gone.

That God who proclaimed "Behold, I make all things new" challenges us on this knife-thin edge of time which we glibly call New Year's Day. Here we are caught between that which has already happened all along the corridors of all time, including our own. And we cannot settle for it as an unredeemed past. There has been too much suffering, too much dreaming, too many trips to Golgotha. Some angel needs to break upon our despairing, saying, "Why search among the dead for one who lives?" Try to answer that question today and you're out on some new roads where there's a possibility of some new travelers reporting, "Did we not feel our hearts on fire as he talked with us on the road?"

A sermon for New Year's Day? Each person becomes that sermon, hopefully moving with newness into that future which can be altered by our decisions. Dag Hammarskjöld, that mystic Secretary General of the United Nations, penned this prayer: "For all that has been—Thanks. For all that is to be—Yes!" It is a prayer which springs from a faith which knows that in the beginning was the Word. We beheld his glory as of the only-begotten. He was the light, and the darkness cannot put it out. That makes us stand taller and truly wish to one another, "A Happy New Year!"

# HE TAUGHT US HOW TO LOVE

*Andrew J. Young, Jr.*

*Congressman, Fifth Congressional District,
Atlanta, Georgia*

So much could have been different had not Martin Luther King, Jr.'s heart been stilled on that infamous day in Memphis. He never would have allowed this nation to forget its calling, nor to delude itself into thinking that there was little or no difference between Richard Nixon and Hubert Humphrey in '68. He would have refused to interpret the death of more than fifty-five thousand American sons in an immoral war as "achieving peace." The years of revolutionary rhetoric and frustration politics might have been better spent, and perhaps we would be much further down the road toward the realization of his dream of universal brotherhood.

But even in death, Martin made his humble contributions. He gave more to this nation in thirty-nine years than many men, of equal talent, could ever give. He broke the silent terror of McCarthyism in Montgomery in 1955 and gave voice to the plaintive longing for justice in the hearts of ten million southern black Americans. He taught us how to love and pointed us in the direction of equality without ever giving in to hatred. He promulgated a method of change that thrived on an organized aggressive goodwill which confronted evil and refused to be drawn into its web of complicity. He demonstrated that "truth" (a deeper understanding of man's conflicts) and "love" (a systematic attack on specific injustice while forgiving all those involved by tradition or weakness) can be mobilized into beautiful, world-changing forces.

He never despaired of his commitment to nonviolence, but he would despair of his inability to overcome the violence-prone nature of our society. He dared to confront a nation whose total orientation had been toward violence—cops and robbers, cowboys

10

and gunslingers, bloodletting and death, a $70 billion Pentagon budget—with the notion that the human soul and mind are even more powerful than atomic weapons. His organization and message never had more than a few hundred thousand dollars, yet he turned around an entire nation in Birmingham with a staff of only fourteen. Had it not been for those efforts, the southern states might have been a bitter and bloody battlefield that would make Irish violence pale in comparison.

Even today, his life cries out to us. His warning, "nonviolence or nonexistence," has been heard by millions who are now ready to say, "I ain't gonna study war no more."

One would think that such a man would be unanimously acclaimed by his fellow men, yet his life and words were constantly harassed by those who would veil themselves in the authority of government. The FBI spread malicious gossip, tapped his phones, and bugged his places of residence long before it became fashionable. Ironically, he was informed of this surveillance by both President Kennedy and Attorney General Kennedy. He made no protest and seemed more concerned about their fear than his own vulnerability.

The IRS had him indicted for tax evasion, only to have his case rejected by an all-white jury in Alabama. However, Martin's tax problems were with him until his death. His problem: that he gave away too much of his earnings! The Nobel prize, in excess of fifty thousand dollars, was divided between movement organizations, Morehouse College, and Ebenezer Baptist Church. He would inevitably have to borrow money to pay taxes on money which he had given away. No tax shelter or charity depletion allowances were available to him, and he donated his early papers to Boston University with no consideration of deduction.

Through all the trials and tribulations, his was a beautiful life— the life of a man who belonged to others, the "least of these" in our society.

He would be proud of the progress we have made politically. The election of black mayors in Los Angeles, Detroit, Raleigh, Atlanta, and more than a thousand elected officials in the South alone are a fulfillment of an important part of his dream. It is not generally realized that his movement stressed the obtaining of the ballot; Martin spent more time working on behalf of voting rights than any other issue. The most important civil rights legislation of the century was the product of his 1965 Selma movement. Those of us elected in majority white districts indicate not only a growth of new black voting strengths, but also an indication of white progress beyond the heritage of racism.

He would be thrilled by the broadened ranks of citizen groups who seek to perfect our government through protest, investigation, and legal action—American citizens who are finally learning the truth that blacks have sung since slavery in the spiritual, "Freedom is a constant struggle, we've struggled so long that we must be free."

Martin would see fulfillment of his oft-quoted prophecies in Watergate. "The moral arc of the universe is long, but it bends toward justice"; "Evil cannot permanently organize, for it bears within it the seeds of its own destruction." I can hear his melodious oratory painting impeachment as steeped in patriotism.

His faith in America and the world was a faith "in spite of." He saw us stumbling toward a better way of life in spite of our weakness and perversity. He knew the goodwill which is buried deep within us all, and he worked faithfully to create situations which would allow those good intentions to be translated into good behavior through social and legal reform.

The big question, the economic question, which he raised in the Poor People's Campaign on the eve of his murder, is still the problem confronting America. No longer is it just the question of the poor or the untrained minorities. "We are all bound together in a single garment of destiny, caught in an inescapable network of mutuality." The very fabric of our society is being torn asunder by the greed and corruption of a few—that selfsame few that would shield themselves in the cloak of governmental authority.

"The people who sat in darkness have seen a great light," quoted Martin. "Our only hope today lies in our ability to recapture the revolutionary spirit and go out into a sometimes hostile world declaring eternal hostility to poverty, racism, and militarism. With this powerful commitment, we shall boldly challenge the status quo and unjust mores and thereby speed the day when 'every valley shall be exalted, and every mountain and hill shall be made low, and the crooked shall be made straight and the rough places plain.' "

Martin Luther King's birthday is one of many candles that still shine out of the darkness of his death, to fascinate and glow, illumine and warm.  Above all, he taught us how to love.

# REFLECTIONS ON FREEDOM

*Arnold F. Keller, Jr.*

*Senior Pastor, Lutheran Church of the Reformation, Washington, D.C.*

Our country pauses on this day remembering two distinguished American presidents, two men who are watershed figures in the history of our country, George Washington and Abraham Lincoln. Simply to speak their names is to turn the mind back to crisis points in the hours of birth and the years of the growth of our nation. How does one honor famous men? To honor them in the best way is not to talk so much about things they did as to speak of the ideals for which they lived. Because I believe that this is so, and in this spirit, I offer some thoughts on the subject of freedom.

Perhaps no other idea, no other concept, says so much about the spirit out of which our nation was given birth and so much about what we as a nation would like to stand for today as the concept of freedom and liberty. Of all the qualities by which we would like to be known, of which we would like to say, "This is America," the quality of freedom, of liberty, heads the list.

Many times we recall with pride that two centuries ago the leaders of a yet embryonic nation asserted that all men were entitled to "life, liberty, and the pursuit of happiness." And we sing about ourselves as the "sweet land of liberty." And we listen as our children quote the remarkable words of Lincoln's Gettysburg Address reminding us that this nation was "conceived in liberty." And we remember the fact that when France gave us the Statue of Liberty (note its very name) there were inscribed upon it words of welcome to the "huddled masses, yearning to be free." Waves upon waves of immigrants have sailed into New York Harbor, past that statue, anxious to participate in the freedoms of a New World.

But rhetoric which simply recites the past in glowing phrases, appealing as it may appear, is to be avoided assiduously. An

14

intelligent and meaningful discussion of freedom for us, who are both Americans and Christians, must move from the past to the realities of the present. We have always to think about and talk about freedom in the context of today.

Two examples out of recent American history suggest what I mean. On the one hand, recall the issue raised up a few years ago by the newspaper publication of excerpts from the so-called Pentagon Papers. Whatever else may have been involved, the action focused new attention upon the long cherished principle of freedom of the press (or freedom of access to information). And all of this viewed against the backdrop of the power of men in authority to control the flow of information according to what they declared to be the national interest! The issues were joined, and they were vital ones. In the long run, Judge Murray A. Gurfein's eloquent words penetrated to the heart of the case: "...the security of the nation is not at the ramparts alone. Security also lies in the value of free institutions. A cantankerous press, an obstinate press, a ubiquitous press, must be suffered by those in authority in order to preserve the even greater values of freedom of expression and the right of the people to know."

On the other hand there is our heightened sensitivity to and awareness of intrusions upon personal privacy by gratuitous surveillance measures. To be watched, scrutinized (without at the least being aware of what is happening), and then to be stored away in a computer for recall when needed or wanted, is somehow to be reminded how uncomfortably close to 1984 we have come.

These are illustrations, then, of the context within which alert and concerned people must address themselves to the issues of freedom today. And with that contemporary background let us explore the meaning of freedom from our stance as Christians. For I believe that from our particular understandings about life, we have some important contributions to make to America today. Let me suggest four of them.

Jesus once reminded his disciples that a man's freedom and his commitment to truth go hand in hand. "You will know the truth, and the truth will make you free" (John 8:32). It is a sentence charged with meanings. At the very least it says this:

Openness, honesty, integrity, truthfulness are essential qualities among men, if freedom is to be maintained. Whenever we conceal truth from one another, the dark cloud of mistrust blows across the scene and with it the increased disinclination to permit the existence of a free community. That's the least that Jesus is suggesting. And more? Is he not also talking about his truth, the insights of his teaching and of his message? The truth which Jesus brings us focuses light upon life's real values and very quickly reveals what is phony and worthless; the truth which Jesus brings helps us to get our priorities in the right order, our values clarified. And so, from our stance as Christians we submit that human freedom is strengthened and its possibilities expanded when men have a commitment to truth.

A second consideration is this: Freedom grows out of a belief in the worth and dignity of man. Thus it is that we understand our own personal freedom only in relationship to every other man's freedoms. I affirm what I believe to be my own rights only in the context of affirming the rights of my brother man.

This idea has been and must continue to be the motivating force in our concern for civil liberties. There can be no real freedom for me as long as my brother's rights as a human being are limited, circumscribed, or denied. But the logic of this principle is compelling in the whole arena of the struggle for human rights—not only in the area of civil rights. The Christian who is committed to the dignity of man is called to serve as a mediator between the powerful and the powerless in this world. The Christian shall become the advocate for and the voice of the oppressed when they have no other advocate, no other voice. Granted, this is not a popular role; it wins antagonists more than it wins friends. Yet, if he believes in the worth, the dignity of man, he cannot simply go on propounding platitudes one after another; instead he must act. He must be counted on the side of the poor to plead their case and to make known the claims of justice.

Within the complexities of our society, these kinds of issues are always before us. Perhaps, in today's world, increasingly before us! So, freedom is not just my freedom. It is always the freedom and the rights of my neighbor, my brother. I cannot talk about freedom with any integrity without grounding my life in a genuine belief in the innate worth of every person, without committing myself in his behalf.

Now, a third consideration is one which lies behind the words of Jesus when he said, "Render therefore to Caesar the things that are Caesar's, and to God the things that are God's" (Matt. 22:21). Here we find Jesus giving expression to the principle that while human institutions are "indeed" important, the highest loyalty of which a person is capable is loyalty to God. So it is that we state unequivocally that freedom and a respect for conscience are mutually inclusive ideas; they belong together, never apart. A person, to be truly free, must be free to say no as well as to say yes to his community, to his nation.

Many years ago Stephen Decatur offered his now famous toast. "Our country," he declared. "In her intercourse with foreign nations, may she always be right; but our country, right or wrong." With all of its patriotic fervor and emotion and drama that sentiment cannot be accepted by anyone who takes seriously another and older command: "You shall have no other gods before me."

To be sure it has been the consistent teaching of the Church that the state is an order of God to which the Christian owes definite loyalties and duties. Unfortunately, however, we have frequently bent over backward, even off balance, to elaborate the principle. So much so, in fact, that a German theologian commenting on a catechism in the 1890s wrote this sentence: "It is true then that cruel and despotic rulers . . . and wild conquerors come from God." Clearly a frightful exaggeration of the basic premise!

When Jesus held the coin before his hearers, he was saying something like this: The conscientious citizen must always recognize the place of the state in the divine scheme of things. The authorities do have claims upon the citizen which, under the claims of God, are to be met for the good of the total community. But we have learned in the dark years of the twentieth century that an unquestioning loyalty to a nation state (or for that matter to any of man's institutions) can lead only to disaster. The embarrassing political questions must be asked. The critical citizen is, therefore, the best kind of patriot. So, the Christian insists upon a freedom which respects conscience and belief.

But when the Christian talks about freedom he must explore one idea which is even more basic than these three. Jesus proposed it in the Sermon on the Mount in these words: "No man can serve two masters" (Matt. 6:24). Paul reminded his readers of the same fact: "You belong to the power you choose to obey" (Rom. 6:16). What they were suggesting was this: There is one freedom basic to the life and destiny of every person; it is the freedom to choose one's master. Once that freedom is exercised, it shapes all other choices to come. In a sense, once that choice is made, all future freedom is limited.

In the parable of the empty house Jesus talked about a life swept clean of evil, but still uncommitted to good. The basic choice for the positive is not made, so the negative returns, takes over, and destroys. The point is obvious. Every one of us is mastered by, controlled by, some ideology, some set of overarching principles, some philosophy, some person. Once the basic choice of a master has been made, once that basic freedom is exercised, then a person's politics, his economics, his family relations, his social philosophy, all will be affected and influenced by that choice.

But for whom will that choice be made? Political groups, once in power, corrupted by power, have a way of craving for more power. The dictator demands and must have total obedience. His power depends upon taking power away from others. In doing this he will not respect persons; he will destroy and enslave. He takes a man's freedom and leaves him only servitude.

Jesus also asks for total obedience. But in return he gives purpose, a sense of life's direction. He gives life! In effect Jesus also wants us to be slaves. Did not Paul refer to himself as a slave of the Lord Jesus Christ? Slaves, but heirs as well! For in return he gives us dignity, integrity, power, and thus the freedom to fulfill our potential as persons.

So, we choose a master, or, if you prefer, we decide what it is that we are going to live by. And this is the basic choice that matters, for the rest of our lives are lived according to the master whom we choose to serve.

It is with principles like these that Christian citizens must participate in the political scene, must engage in the ongoing political dialogue. If religious men and women do not call attention to the dimensions of the spiritual, who else will speak? We echo the remarkable words of Felix Morley: "The Spiritual strength of the Republic will not be automatically or mechanically renewed. Spring will return to this land of liberty, not with the vernal equinox, but with the vitality of restored ideals."*

* Felix Morley, *The Power in the People* (New York: Nash Publishing Corp., 1972), p. 243.

# RELIGIOUS FAITH AND POLITICS

*George McGovern*
*United States Senator, South Dakota*

As most of you know, I have been a seminarian and student pastor, and I have also been a teacher. Both of those callings have stayed with me. Some observers think my speeches sound too much like lectures, and others think they sound like sermons.

Whether those qualities are a strength or a weakness I cannot say. But I hope we share the conviction that such traditions have an important place in our public life—that a public servant must teach and learn from the people in constant dialogue, and that a public official must witness to moral principle as he works for particular policies.

A few years ago I read a radio sermon delivered by the Reverend Joel Nederhood of "The Back to God Hour," broadcast from Chicago. The sermon was about the faith of our politicians. Dr. Nederhood contended that Americans have adopted the dangerous custom of separating their morality from their evaluation of their leaders. He said: "To suggest that one's faith might influence a person in his discharge of public office, apparently, is akin to suggesting that the man is guilty of dishonorable conflict of interest. Thus, while candidates for public office often claim some kind of membership in a religious body, they ordinarily disavow any connection between their faith and their views of public policy."

I believe this is wrong for a nation whose founders were so deeply motivated by religious conviction.

We all stand for the constitutional principle of separation of church and state. But we should all stand against the distortion of this principle into the practice of separating our religious faith from politics. For the Bible teaches that government is to serve man, not that men are the servants of government. When the New Testament speaks of "honoring those in authority," for in-

stance, it points out that power is ordained by God for the purpose
of doing good for the people. In this light, I have come to understand the responsibility of political office and the opportunities for
service which it holds.

But we must also recognize a central fact: All that we seek in
our society will not come solely from government. The greatest
challenges of our age defy purely political answers.

I remember the civil rights march of 1963, which was followed
by the historic passage of the Civil Rights Act a year later. Many
Americans hoped that this single act would set us on a rapid
course toward the extinction of racial prejudice. But the real
crisis was still ahead of us—and it is still unresolved. In the last
decade we have learned that discrimination is rooted in attitudes,
and frustrations, and fears that cannot be dispelled by law, but in
our hearts. There is much that can and must be done by government; but much more must be done by each of us in our own
lives.

Our deepest problems are within us—not as an entire people,
but as individual persons. So Christians have a responsibility to
speak to the questions of the spirit which ultimately determine the
state of the material world. Most Americans yearn for meaning
and value in life. This is a preeminent task for those who are in
the church—but it cannot be separated from what happens outside
the church.

Some Christians believe that we are condemned to live with
man's inhumanity to man—with poverty, war, and injustice—and
that we cannot end these evils because they are inevitable.

But I have not found that view in the Bible.

Changed men can change society, and the words of Scripture
clearly assign to us the ministry and the mission of change.

While we know that the kingdom of God will not come from a
politician's platform, we also know if someone is hungry, we
should give him food; if he is thirsty, we should give him drink; if
he is a stranger, we should take him in; if he is naked, we should
clothe him; if he is sick, we should care for him; and if he is in
prison we should visit him. "For inasmuch as you have done it
unto the least of these my brethren, you have done it unto me"

(Matt. 25:40). That is what Scripture says. None of us can be content until all of us are made whole.

This is also the lesson in the lives of the great evangelists. Jonathan Edwards is remembered for his role in the Great Awakening that swept colonial America. But few realize that he was so dedicated to the struggle against suffering and disease that he offered himself to test a smallpox vaccine. In this act of charity and love and sacrifice, he died.

John Wesley set up clinics to bring medical care to the deprived citizens of London. And in the 1800s, one of the great evangelists, William Wilberforce, was a leader in the abolitionist movement, fighting for human freedom.

The most notable advances of the eighteenth and nineteenth centuries—the fight for decent labor conditions and against slavery, and the efforts for prison reform—seemed to flow from the evangelical tides in society which preceded and accompanied them. Breakthroughs occurred in overcoming inhumanity and injustice because individuals had become infused with a compassion for others—and, even more than that, because the conscience of the nation had been touched and enlivened.

Today, the conscience of our nation must be touched anew.

Arnold Toynbee has written that all the great civilizations of history have fallen, not to conquering armies from without, but to a deterioration of spirit from within. Toynbee asserts that America "now stands for what Rome stood for." I believe that is so in many ways. America, too, is a country of enormous wealth. Our people, like the ancient Romans, seem to live more and more for materialistic satisfaction. Standards of morality and precious values are in disarray, as they were then.

This is the real meaning of the Watergate scandal. It is a lie that our politics is as bad as some men made it in 1972. It is a libel that all our leaders have been lawbreakers. Yet the moral blindness which brought us Watergate has also brought a host of other evils, the common works of a callous neglect.

Therefore, as we sit in judgment now upon others attempting to decide fairly the truth about individual innocence or guilt, in crime and cover-up, we must also sit in judgment upon ourselves, attempting to see truly our country as it is. In this sense, Watergate is not just the tragedy of some men, but the trial of a whole society. We must learn from it the larger lessons of moral life—that government, too, must be guided by faith, that we must have a fundamental stirring of our moral and spiritual values.

Such an awakening can free us from a relentless devotion to material affluence with too much for some citizens and too little for others. It can free us from a blind trust in armed might. It can free us from a dogmatic faith in salvation through technology.

Such an awakening can stir our compassion for others, restore the commitment of our hearts to right what is wrong among us, and revive the values that alone can guide our lives and give us happiness.

We must look into our souls to find the way out of the crisis of our society. As was so often true for the people of God in biblical days, we must heed the words of the prophets.

The New Testament tells us, "Be not conformed to the world, but be you transformed by the renewing of your minds" (Rom. 12:2). Some Christians have misused this passage as a pretext for isolation from the existence around us. But the point is that our thinking, our perspectives, and our actions should not be molded by the world's view and its tides of opinion; rather, they are to be rooted in God's vision. And we must carry the good news of that vision into the world.

America was founded as part of a spiritual pilgrimage. It was born in a noble vision of human existence. The first settlers named their land New England because they hoped to found a new order. Our forebears inscribed the great seal of the United States with the words, "a new order for the ages." And on that seal, a pyramid, which stands for material wealth, supports a symbol which stands for spiritual strength.

In 1630, John Winthrop preached a sermon on the deck of the Arabella to the first settlers. He said: "We shall be as a city upon a hill, the eyes of all people upon us; so that if we shall deal falsely with our God in this work we have undertaken and so cause him to withdraw his present help from us; we shall be made a story and a by-word through the world."

I believe we can still deal truly, and righteously, with the great gifts that have been ours since the time the Puritans reached these shores. But this will come only after a struggle that touches all our hearts, and is resolved there.

The prophet gives us God's promise: "If my people, which are called by my name, shall humble themselves, and pray, and seek my face, and turn from their wicked ways; then will I hear from heaven, and will forgive their sin, and will heal their land" (2 Chron. 7:14).

So what then do we do? What is your responsibility, and what is mine? Micah asked and answered the same question in a verse I have remembered since my childhood, and turned back to ever since: "What doth the Lord require of Thee, but to do justly, and to love mercy, and to walk humbly with thy God?" (Mic. 6:8).

# ON LAW IN HUMAN LIFE

*Mulford Q. Sibley*

*Professor of Political Science, University of Minnesota, Minneapolis, Minnesota*

And all the people gathered as one man into the square before the Water Gate; and they told Ezra the scribe to bring the book of the law of Moses which the Lord had given to Israel. And Ezra the priest brought the law before the assembly, both men and women and all who could hear with understanding, on the first day of the seventh month. And he read from it facing the square before the Water Gate from early morning until midday, in the presence of the men and the women and those who could understand; and the ears of all the people were attentive to the book of the law.                                  Neh. 8:1–3

But this is the covenant which I will make with the house of Israel after those days, says the Lord: I will put my law within them, and I will write it upon their hearts; and I will be their God, and they shall be my people.                                  Jer. 31:33

"For the Son of man goes as it has been determined; but woe to that man by whom he is betrayed!" ... And he said to them, "The kings of the Gentiles exercise lordship over them; and those in authority over them are called benefactors."                                  Luke 22:22, 25

But Peter and the apostles answered, "We must obey God rather than men."                                  Acts 5:29

Law has played a complex and controversial role in human existence and continues to do so today. In our own time, as in every generation, there are those who call for more "law and order." Sometimes we are told that the law is sacred. On other occasions, however, it is said that "the law is an ass."

Law, like all institutions, has many sides and can be approached in many ways. After one has reflected on its role in human life, one often emerges with much dissatisfaction and many unanswered questions.

Our texts for today give some impression of the many ways in which law and our attitudes to it can be approached. In the passage from Nehemiah, the returning Hebrew exiles begin their efforts to reconstruct the community by listening to a reading of the Law of Moses before the water gate. It is a solemn occasion and they realize that without the law—which embodies their religious and ethical code as well as much of their criminal and civil law—they cannot succeed. For Jeremiah, the problem is one of internalizing the commands of the law, thus eliminating external penalties; and he foresees a day when human beings will observe the law solely because they realize that it is right to do so. The last two texts pose the vexing issue of whether we should obey law under all circumstances: Jesus tells us that we should recognize a legitimate sphere for Caesar but also a very important one for God. Peter and the apostles, brought before the high priest for violating legal commands of the ecclesiastical establishment, maintain that in the event of conflict between laws of God and laws of men, the former must take precedence.

What can we say by way of elaboration on the texts? Let us first comment on the nature and purpose of law, then remind ourselves of man's contradictory and ambivalent attitudes, and, finally, touch on the problem of obedience.

Sometimes the term "law" is used descriptively. Thus we speak of "scientific laws" when we wish to designate the supposed regularities of nature. The "law of gravity" does not tell us what we ought to do. Instead, it tells us what will happen if we behave in certain ways. We cannot "violate" the law of gravity.

In this sermon, however, we are not concerned with law as *describing* some regularity but rather with law *prescribing* norms or standards for human conduct. Law in this sense has been defined in many ways. Thus some have seen it primarily as an expression of reason. Thomas Aquinas, for example, does not even refer to "force" in his definition: "law is an ordinance of reason for the common good made by him who has the care of the community, and promulgated." By way of contrast, others view "force" as central to what they term law. Are the rules of churches and trade unions to be regarded as law? Some say yes, while others reply no. There have been those who have seemed to equate law with custom, or have thought of it in some sense as an expression of custom. One school holds it to be a kind of deposit of the history of a people. The positivist would sharply distinguish law from morality, identifying the former with the command of the human ruler of the state. On the other hand, some view legitimate human law as an expression of natural law, which is a general system of reasoning and morality not created by any human ruler.

While all thinkers speak of the sanctions of law—that is, methods for ensuring that the law is obeyed—those sanctions need not take any particular form. Thus the ultimate sanction for church law is the expulsion of a member who disobeys it. Fines, too, and monetary civil penalties are forms of sanctions. And one's conscience can be a sanction: One will be distraught and experience spiritual anguish if one does not follow the law.

Perhaps we can say that there is an element of validity in many conceptions of law but that each, too, is subject to limitations. Thus most legal systems make much of rationality, and the defenders of law would say that it seeks the common good. In fact, though, many laws may not reflect the common good. If the decree of a ruler appears to be "rational" (itself a word of several meanings) but lacks support in the community, is it truly law? Conundrums of this kind bother the jurists of various schools of thought. Or again: Does a statute on the books which is not enforced have the force of a law which I must obey?

Law would seem to arise out of our status as human beings. We exist midway between the angels and the beasts: The former do not need to develop law either through custom or legislation, for presumably they are so close to God that they are ordered without law; the beasts, on the other hand, do not require what we call law because they are largely controlled by instincts or at least innate tendencies. Man, by contrast, has neither the guidance of the angels nor the instinctual equipment of the beasts. He is both free and social and therefore develops legal structures to provide a framework for his freedom and an order for expressing his sociality. In general, it might be said that without a legal ordering of some kind, the actions of each of us might become arbitrary and harmful to others, even though in general each might wish the others well. In a sense, some law is an appeal from Philip drunk (Philip temporarily without his normal concern for others and his rationality) to Philip sober (what Philip would be if he fully expressed his social nature and his rationality).

Sometimes laymen make the mistake of thinking that all law is criminal law—perhaps because so much attention is given to it in the media, especially through stories about violence against human beings. But law takes a multitude of forms—constitutional, torts (or civil wrongs), contracts, administrative (a rapidly expanding field because of the growing complexity of administrative structures), and others.

Sometimes, too, we think of law as opposed to liberty. But this is not necessarily so, at least in net effect. Law and freedom may be related positively to each other, as when law regulates traffic (how much freedom would we have in driving if there were no rules for traffic?), protects our freedom of speech and the press, and enlarges the rights of minorities through fair employment practices legislation.

In short, law has been, in many respects, one of the central institutions of what we call civilization.

Yet it is also true that human beings have been ambivalent and uncertain about it. On the one hand, they have denounced it and its practitioners: Thus Plato compares it to "an ignorant tyrant"; many utopias try to exclude law and lawyers, or at least to reduce their influence; Jeremy Bentham, attacking the lawyers even though he himself was one, said that the most difficult task on earth was to turn an English lawyer into an honest man! On the other hand, law has at times been glorified, even by those who have criticized it: Thus Plato thought of it as indispensable for human life, given the fact that there are no perfectly righteous men to serve as rulers; and our libraries are filled with encomiums on particular systems of law—the common law, for instance, or the Roman law.

How do the critics deal with law? First of all, they suggest, law must necessarily put human beings and situations into categories and this will often lead to injustice, since no two human beings or situations are exactly alike. This is one reason Plato thought law was deficient: It was always trying to make things "one" which were not one. Thus it was a kind of tyranny. Secondly, as Marxists and others point out, law is often used as an instrument by ruling classes to serve their own rather than the public interest. Under these circumstances, law as actually administered will often punish blacks more severely than whites for the same offense, and poor people more harshly than the elite. In a broad sense, too, law is the instrument through which wealth is distributed unfairly under cover of so-called "justice." The lawyer historically has often been seen as an agent of the wealthy against the poor or the middle classes.

While much of this criticism of the law and its administration is valid, still the defenders of law also have a plausible case. Although they might admit the possible injustice of fitting unique human beings and unique situations into the rather rigid categories of law, still they would maintain that without such legal guidelines established before the conflict arises, human beings would probably be subject to the caprice of despots. Law may be a cumbrous device for shielding us against despotism, but experience would seem to show that it is one of the better instruments we have. Moreover, systems of "equity" jurisdiction which correct some of these injustices tend to arise even though it may be true that "equity" also takes on some of the undesirable characteristics of law. The defender of law might point out, too, that although law and the administration of law do quite frequently reflect the interests of the ruling classes, still they at least aspire to universality and impartiality and this aspiration acts as something of a goad to limit their employment as devices for undergirding the rich and the powerful.

There are many instances where the rich, the elite, and the unruly mob have been restricted by law in their tendency to exploit and manipulate the poor and the powerless. Rights to freedom of speech and religion of such minorities as Jehovah's witnesses, for example, have been sustained by law as administered by the courts.

Admittedly, of course, the situation is mixed. Reformers have many things to do before the goal of "equal justice under law," in its broadest sense, is reached. We need, for instance, a revolution in the economic order—one which will distribute wealth and income much more equitably than today—before we can truly bridge the gap between aspiration and actuality. The defender of law might also suggest that one reason many of us may be highly critical of law is that we expect it to do too much, especially in the area of criminal law. The law by its nature is limited in what it can do. Law cannot in itself make men love one another, for example, and it is a very unsatisfactory instrument for regulating sexual conduct. Perhaps if we would repeal many of our laws which go beyond what law can do, we would promote respect for the law in what it *can* do.

Let us conclude by asking an ancient question: Do we have an obligation to obey law under all circumstances?

Anyone having prophetic religious convictions will have to reply: "Of course not." In any conflict between what he regards as God's will and the earthly ruler's decrees, the religious person will side with Peter: "We ought to obey God rather than men." Each of us has an obligation to decide whether or not to obey; and if we do not accept this responsibility, we are rejecting the freedom with which God has endowed us.

Although conformity to law is an important value and, in general, we should obey as a mark of respect for the society which helped to make us what we are, obedience to human law is not the only value. At times, in the event of conflict, we may have to give precedence to other human obligations, to moral standards which may contradict a particular law, or to duties to God.

Generations of human beings have rightly rejected the proposition that we ought to obey all laws, regardless of their nature. Those who before the Civil War sheltered fugitive slaves in defiance of fugitive slave laws, who in World War I accepted tortures in prison because they could not in conscience go to war, who defined the ostensibly legal orders of Hitler's minions, or who committed civil disobedience during the civil rights struggle correctly concluded that there are times when we may have an obligation to *disobey* law.

Just as we should *obey* law *on principle*, and not because a policeman is near or because we fear a penalty, so on occasion we may have to disobey for a moral principle, as did the early Christian.

Both principled obedience and principled disobedience show reverence for law and are marks of the morally developed soul. Both take law seriously in that they judge it at the bar of that most precious achievement of man—a tender and thoughtful conscience.

# OUR ONLY SECURITY

*John M. Swomley, Jr.*

*Professor of Social Ethics, St. Paul School of Theology, Kansas City, Missouri*

The world in which we live is a world with many national armed forces. The nations of the world together spend a total of almost $250 billion a year on their military establishments, which represents a heavy tax burden for many people. Each nation has developed ways of encouraging the people to support its armed forces. One way is the setting aside of a special day for this purpose.

In the United States the first celebration of Armed Forces Day was in 1950, but for many years before that there had been an Army Day and also a Navy Day whose purposes were to build civilian support for those two branches of the military establishment.

When we celebrate Armed Forces Day we have to ask ourselves what we mean by the armed forces. Is it a huge impersonal war machine, or is it a group of flesh and blood human beings, most of whom don't want war? Listen to this sentence from a letter sent by a nineteen-year-old soldier to the mother of a schoolmate killed in Vietnam: "Maybe someday all the sorrow and lives that are lost every day over here will show people that there is nothing to come out of war. . . ." (*Kansas City Star*, 26 May 1975).

Recently I asked a retired Regular Army General how he thought the church might observe Armed Forces Day. He said: "There is only one way to honor those in the armed forces—by exposing the true nature of war so that everyone will realize that peace is a necessity. Civilians can honor soldiers by making sure they will never again be called to kill and be killed in war. Take the Bible seriously where it says, 'Beat your swords into plowshares.' "

Peace has always been desirable, but the reason the general spoke of it as a necessity today is the destructiveness of nuclear war. In our day the most striking fact about the armed forces is not the young men and women who have enlisted, but the terrible destructive power of the weapons. A single Polaris submarine missile has the explosive power of one million tons of TNT, or as much destructive power as was dropped on Germany during World War II. There are sixteen such missiles on each Polaris submarine!

Secretary of Defense Robert McNamara was asked at a congressional hearing in 1963 what would be the military situation after a nuclear exchange between the United States and the Soviet Union. He said:

> This is a question we have considered. And I can't answer it. I think probably the fatalities in western Europe would approach 90 million, the fatalities in the United States would approach 100 million [later his computer increased this to 149 million dead] and the fatalities in the Soviet Union would approach 100 million. Now when you consider on the order of 300 million dead in these areas it is very difficult to conceive of what kind of military weapons would continue to exist. . . . We have none the less faced that issue, and we have systems provided that we believe would survive. But it exceeds the extent of imagination to conceive of how those forces might be used and of what benefit they would be to our nation at that point.

We know that if the United States were to use its arsenal of nuclear weapons against the Soviet Union and if all the weapons of that country were to be destroyed so that there was no retaliation, we Americans would nevertheless be destroyed by the radioactivity from our own weapons which the air currents would carry to us.

The first thing we can say about nuclear war is that it is impossible to eliminate our enemies without risking our own extinction. In other words, war destroys those it was designed to defend as well as those it was intended to destroy.

The second thing we can say about nuclear war is that it reveals God's will about organized violence. Just as the nature of an oak tree is more evident in its full development than it is in the acorn, so the destructiveness of nuclear war reveals more fully God's indictment of armed force than was evident in the use of swords and spears. Yet centuries ago the Hebrew prophets proclaimed to their nation that God willed peace. Both Isaiah and Micah looked forward to the day when people would beat their swords into plowshares and their spears into pruning hooks.

The third thing we can say about war is that through nuclear weapons God is confronting the human race with a life or death decision. In effect, God is saying: "You humans have been unwilling voluntarily to form a worldwide human community but have organized yourselves into armed nations. Now you have a choice between world community or nuclear destruction." If the instinct of race preservation is still present in the human species, God is in effect coercing us through the fact of nuclear weapons to abolish war and achieve reconciliation with our enemies.

The facts about nuclear war indicate that peace is a necessity. Nevertheless many persons in and out of the armed forces believe that the manufacture and stockpile of nuclear weapons is actually the best way to prevent war. This theory of deterrence is based on the assumption that if each nation is able to destroy its opponent, neither side will dare to attack. Nuclear deterrence therefore means that the entire civilian population of another nation is treated as a hostage for the conduct of its armed forces. This is the reverse of the golden rule: "Be prepared to do unto others what you *don't* want them to do unto you, and they won't do it."

The first problem with this theory of deterrence is its incredible stupidity and brutality. Instead of trying to win people in other nations by policies that would encourage them not to seek our destruction, we tell them that their total population is targeted for destruction in the event of war. Even the *opponents* of the regimes we dislike thereby become our targeted enemies rather than our friends.

The second problem with the theory of deterrence is that it does not rule out war by accident. The United States now has about thirty thousand nuclear weapons. More than half of these are stationed overseas in other countries or are on the high seas. There is always the danger that these weapons might be seized.

During the warfare in 1975 between Greek and Turkish troops over Cyprus, a concerned U.S. soldier wrote to Senator Stuart Symington about the nuclear warheads stored in Greece and Turkey, expressing fear that these nations might seize these weapons to use against each other. He wrote: "No more than 4 to 6 U.S. soldiers guard the bunkers which store the nukes! Most of the troops (about 40 per detachment) are housed about a quarter of a mile from the bunkers and could be easily isolated from the warheads."

The third problem with deterrence is that it does not prevent action by terrorist groups. The Center for Defense Information reports that there is serious danger of theft or hijacking of nuclear weapons by terrorist groups. There are more than fifty major terrorist groups around the world and thousands of nuclear weapons deployed by British, French, Russian, and American forces, some under questionable security conditions.

There is also danger from the people who handle nuclear weapons. About 120,000 persons have access to U.S. weapons or material used to make them. During a single year 3,647 persons with access to nuclear weapons were removed from their jobs after it was discovered that they had mental illness or were involved in alcoholism, drug abuse, or other similar problems. An average of three persons per thousand in the U.S. armed forces suffer from mental illness serious enough to require professional care.

Insofar as deterrence works, it rests on the assumption that the leaders of the nations that possess nuclear weapons are rational people who will recognize the destructive power of these weapons and therefore avoid war. But if they are rational we can negotiate with them, make treaties with them, and persuade them that trade in food, natural resources, and other products is an inducement for peace. We can persuade them that the money and resources all of us spend on armaments would increase our total wealth if it were spent on houses and schools and machinery that would improve our standard of living.

In the final analysis, we can honor our men and women in the armed forces by respecting their desire for life, liberty, and happiness. But this means concern for the well-being of those in other

lands.  Eugene Carson Blake, who has served both the National
Council of Churches and the World Council of Churches, has
written: "In World War II we were asked to regard as the ultimate
fiends of humanity the Germans and the Japanese against whom
we fought by the side of our great and good friends, the Russians
and the Chinese.  Today we are asked to regard these same Russians and Chinese as the ultimate fiends and accept the former
fiends as our great and good friends.  We may be stupid, but not
*that* stupid."

There is only one truth, that of Jesus Christ, who said "Love
your enemies,...do good to those that hate you" (Matt. 5:44).
We can respect and honor those in the armed forces only if we
recognize in the people and armed forces of other nations the same
need for peace and freedom that we have.  It is our present fear of
the intentions of other nations rather than any concern for their
well-being that motivates us.  To some degree this is inevitable so
long as nations are organized for war.  During the period between
World War I and World War II the League of Nations asked each
of its member nations what made it necessary for them to maintain
their armed forces at their current size.  A League official said
that the answers of each nation could be summarized in one sentence: "I am anxious to disarm, but my armaments are already as
small as I can safely afford.  I am a peaceful nation, but I am
surrounded by bellicose countries."  The League official concluded that in its own eyes "every nation is a lamb, and every
other nation a wolf."

We must recognize that in the nuclear age the war system is the
enemy, and the peoples of other nations, like ourselves, have nothing to gain by its continuance.  If a nation were completely disarmed and therefore no threat to any nuclear power, there would
be no reason for any nation to want to destroy it.  But if nuclear
war came, that same nation would be destroyed regardless of the
size or effectiveness of its armed force.

When we really believe that we can live as brothers and sisters
with the Russians, the Germans, the Arabs, and the Chinese, we
shall be able to give up our weapons.

A number of years ago an old Indian chief in Arizona was asked about the prospects for world peace. He replied: "Everyone smoke pipe of peace, but nobody inhale." He is right. Most of us give only lip service to peace because we still mistakenly believe we or our nation could somehow survive a nuclear conflagration. We can't! We must learn now the lesson that peace is our only security.

Our task is to become so committed to God and his will for human community that we may share in obtaining the security of a disarmed world.

# THE CELEBRATION OF SORROW

*Robert Cleveland Holland*

*Preaching Minister, Shadyside Presbyterian Church, Pittsburgh, Pennsylvania*

I was born on Memorial Day in the year 1928. The earliest recollections of my birthdays are inextricably interwoven with waving flags and blaring bands and marching soldiers commemorating wars long since fought. I can remember a touring car with two or three ancient Civil War veterans, old men still ambulatory from the Spanish-American War, and company upon company of American Legionnaires—mostly men in their thirties, veterans of World War I trenches—proudly parading down State Street on their way to "Decoration Day" ceremonies in the cemetery.

From the time I was old enough to be conscious of world events —and when was that, when I was six or seven, in 1934 or 1935? —I have heard without ceasing, until this very moment, of wars and rumors of wars. The names of the scenes of violence stain the calendar and bloody the pages of even my short memory: Ethiopia, Spain, China, Austria, Sudetenland, Britain, Dunkirk, Pearl Harbor, Leningrad, Guadalcanal, Normandy, Iwo Jima, Berlin, Hiroshima, China again, Korea, Kenya, Egypt, Israel, Cuba, Vietnam, Laos, Cambodia. And from where will the next name come, inevitably to be added to the endless list?

For a very long time western civilization has, with a subtle sort of innocence, glorified war, and Memorial Day weekend has been America's high holiday of the martial. We have liked the beating of the drums, the sculpting of the victors, the polished precision of West Point and Annapolis. Uniforms and guns, tanks and battleships, bombers and bazookas have fired our adult imaginations and, miniaturized, have fascinated our children as playthings. Even in church we have clothed the Prince of Peace in the trappings of battle garments, and from "Brightly gleams our banner pointing to the sky, waving on Christ's soldiers to their home on high," through "Soldiers of Christ arise," "Onward Christian soldiers," and "Stand up for Jesus, ye soldiers of the cross" to "The Battle Hymn of the Republic" we have not minded one bit forging the cross into the sword.

But that era is ended. As the incredible horrors of conflict have escalated to the crescendo of the unthinkable, at last everyone who is sane hates war, and the world has wearied of its incessant wrestling with weapons. What then are we to do with Memorial Day? What veneration of past human contentiousness can a Christian bring to the graveside of those fallen in arms?

In one of his essays written at the height of "the war to end wars," the Australian F. W. Boreham put forward the theory that in our human makeup, *sorrow must be celebrated*. In his usual picturesque pattern Boreham guides his readers through the galleries of Sydney and Melbourne Art Museums, and proves the point that perhaps the majority of the world's most memorable paintings derive their beauty and their magnetism from the portrayal of suffering. Think how many artists from Dürer to Dali have been almost obsessed with the Crucifixion; has any scene been depicted more often? And not just the world's most monumental suffering which happened that one day at Calvary. The secret of the emotion-inspiring beauty of the best loved among pictures, songs, stories, and even private memories is often their hint of disharmony in a minor key.

Every Christian who enjoys the great hymns of the Church is moved by the melodies which Wales has contributed to worship. Those splendid tunes soar up the mountainsides of Cambria—but they also plunge into the dark valleys of Glamorgan. They praise the love of God, but they also reflect the hunger, hard work, and bleakness of a people who have largely chopped their livelihood out of coal seams in the black depths of sweating mines. They know the need of celebrating sorrow, even in song.

Memorial Day is certainly not a part of the liturgical calendar; it is no church holy day. But perhaps it ought to be. When else do we pause to remember those who in their deaths have given the rest of us the continuation of life? No matter how intensely any

American hates war, it requires unbelievable insensitivity to walk among the marble markers of Arlington or to visit the endless cross-and-star-planted fields of Flanders, "row on row," and not feel a deep emotion of indebtedness to the tens of thousands of all but anonymous names: lives laid down, unwillingly given, because of commitment to a patriotic duty.

An uncle of mine fell in the Battle of the Somme in the Spring of 1918 and was buried in Bony near the site of his death. I shall never forget the feeling that gripped me as I stood by his simple, numbered grave in the well-kept military cemetery in Aisne on my first visit to Europe, thirty-nine years after the gravediggers had completed their grim task. My grandmother (his mother) and my mother (his sister) had adored him as son and brother. His letters home—yellowed, crumbled epistles of lonesomeness and horror, which I have inherited—spoke constantly of his loathing of the trenches, his abhorrence of the idea of killing another human being, his yearning for family and friends and home. But the bullet which struck him down was unknowing of all that, though I'm sure it came from a gun held in the hands of a German boy whose heart knew the same sentiments as my uncle's. I don't quite know how to describe all I felt on that day I stood beside Uncle Will's foreign burial place—that man I had never known, only knew of. But this I do know: Those feelings were vital to my being as a member of the family, and of the human race, and of the body of Christ. A very important part of me would have been left empty had I not undertaken, as part of a journey otherwise dedicated to tourism and pleasure, the pilgrimage in France to celebrate a sorrow—perhaps the first one I ever knew about as a child—a sorrow I had and have lived with all my life.

We need a Memorial Day to remember and to visit the treasured traces of past sorrows.

There is a pathos in the text I have chosen: "So Moses, the servant of the Lord, died there in the land of Moab ... but no man knoweth of his sepulchre unto this day.... And the children of Israel wept for Moses" (Deut. 34:5–8). "No man knoweth of his sepulchre unto this day." There is an implication of loss in the unmarked scene of Moses' burial. Oh, I know all the arguments against emphasizing the decaying mortal remains of the immortal soul. I live in a city whose prominent families of past generations apparently tried to outdo one another in the architectural splendor of their mausoleums which clutter our cemeteries like temples along the Nile. In my own will I have left specific instructions that my body is to be cremated and the ashes disposed of by the funeral undertaker. My purpose is to remind my family and friends that my real self is not somewhere in the ground; rather that I am spiritually at home with God. But I am not altogether certain that I have done the right thing.

On the one hand—owing to that belief—while I loved my father very much, in the twenty-five years since he died I have never visited his graveside even once. On the other hand, I have made extensive trips to meditate and be awed at the sepulchres of Livingstone in Westminster Abbey, of Churchill in Bladon, of Carlisle in Haddington, of Patrick in DownPatrick, of Washington in Mount Vernon, of Hawthorne, Emerson, and Thoreau in Concord. It is an ambivalence of convictions I have. For I shudder at the hopelessness which leads some to the graves of loved ones years after demise to everlastingly grieve, mourn, and leave flowers. At the same time I am thrilled to be hovering over the bones of giants of the past whom I admire. I spent a whole morning wandering, with tears of reverence on my cheeks, in Finsbury's Bunhill Fields where the list of the buried eminent is endless—Watts, Wesley, Bunyan, Defoe, Blake, and literally scores of others, mostly nineteenth century Dissenters. Those tears were the outward symbols of inner feelings I would trade for nothing: the celebration of sorrow.

No, it is not *just* the celebration of sorrow. It is also the celebration of the greatness of world-changing lives, of their genius, of their devotion, of their faith. No one is able to be a fully developed, sensitive person without spending some of time's hours "in the valley of the shadow." But much can be experienced there far beyond the "vale of tears" as Montgomery called it. When I speak of the *celebration* of sorrow, I truly intend the word "celebration" in its accurate meaning. It has been said that the modern Church overuses the word "celebration." I disagree with that criticism. The dictionary offers two rather significant definitions of "celebration": "to honor with appropriate ceremony" and "to demonstrate satisfaction. . . ." There are aspects of sorrow worthy of celebration.

Every pastor has become familiar with the need of the grieving to *express* their grief. It is not beneficial to the healing process of bereavement to keep all the outward demonstrations of sorrow bottled up inside at a time of death and loss. In terms of Webster's definition, sorrow must be honored "with appropriate ceremony." Who is so callous as to contend that tears are out of place at a funeral? Certainly, it may be our own selfish deprivation we are feeling. But that's what sorrow, for a Christian, is all about: When someone we love has gone to be with the Lord, we need waste little grief on the departed. It is being left behind, on the shore, that hurts. And the tears—even more, the tender travail back of the tears—are a demonstration satisfactorily celebrating sorrow.

"The children of Israel wept for Moses." I've often heard my wife lovingly comfort someone who apologized for weeping in her presence by saying, "That's what the Lord gave us tearducts for." In other words, sorrow can be therapeutic. And the celebration of sorrow can produce very positive and useful results. In George Gissing's autobiography, where he proves himself to have received Dickens's mantle of social conscience, he says, writing from his beautiful home in Devon, "Once I should have said that there were certain street names, certain mental images of obscure London, which would make me wretched as often as they came before me. Now I find that part of life interesting and pleasant to look back upon—greatly more so than many subsequent times when I lived amid decencies and had enough to eat." He valued days of privation and distress more than days of plenty and distinction. To look back, to celebrate those painful experiences, was a source of strength—as the book of Genesis puts it when Isaac, now elderly himself, returned to the scenes of his father's sojourn and "dug again the old wells of Abraham" (Gen. 26:18). There is refreshing spiritual water to be drawn from memory's visits to former scenes which may indeed have been agonizing at the time.

Why should a nation mark the passing of the centuries? America glorifies the era of the Revolution, but they were pathetic times for our ancestors who actually lived and died in the racked anxiety of ill-prepared war and immature independence. For some years I lived in Morristown, New Jersey, where Washington wintered his troops twice, in 1777 and 1780. Jockey Hollow National Historical Park there preserves relics of horrible suffering through those frigid months of unrelieved adversity. The unpaid, thinly clothed troops were easy prey to frostbite, pneumonia, depression, and every communicable germ that came along. Among the reconstructed buildings at the park is the crudely fabricated mud and log hospital where the ill lay huddled on damp earthen floors around small fires that succeeded above all in filling the rooms with choking smoke. Even the church of which I later became the minister was turned into an emergency ward for the victims of smallpox in the spring of 1777, and the congregation—those who were well enough—had to worship outdoors. Is it any wonder that the encampment of Pennsylvania's militia mutinied, stole local farmer's horses, and rode off home, sick to death of the hopeless war? And is it not a wonder we won the war, considering the conditions? Of the nine great battles Washington fought, he lost six. But somehow he won the three that mattered most. And now, as America looks back across two centuries to those rugged days, is not the very suffering itself, the very tragicness (if I may coin a word) the building material out of which is constructed the integrity, the honor, the distinction, the importance which we commemorate? We celebrate sorrow, and it is good and valuable that we do.

For a Christian every return to the foot of the cross in praise or prayer, in meditation or motivation, is a Memorial Day—a celebration of sorrow. There our Lord gave his life in a hideous climax of suffering. But when we fondle the cross in our pockets, or hang it around our necks, or raise it atop our steeples, it becomes for us the supreme symbol of rejoicing victory. The cross is the ultimate celebration of sorrow. As Boreham puts it, it is from the cross's pain "that a pain-racked world derives courage and comfort . . . strength and hope, and the life that knows no ending."

Remember how George Matheson celebrated the sudden sorrow

of blindness that robbed all the promises of his youthful ambition? He sat down and composed the haunting poem, "O Love, That Wilt Not Let Me Go." And the last verse says it all:

> O cross that liftest up my head,
> I dare not ask to fly from thee;
> I lay in dust life's glory dead,
> And from the ground there blossoms red
> Life that shall endless be.

# INDEPENDENCE—DEPENDENCE—INTERDEPENDENCE

*Wilton E. Bergstrand*

Pastor, Holy Trinity Lutheran Church,
Jamestown, New York

Each of America's holidays tells us something significant about freedom. And each truth is related to the other; each is vital to the other.

On the Fourth of July we celebrate our *independence* from every form of human tyranny.

In the Declaration of Independence we are given the blueprint of a great dream. The fifty-six signers of the birth certificate of our nation pledged their lives, their fortune, their sacred honor. These were not empty, bombastic phrases. Almost all of the signers lost property; some lost loved ones and gave their own lives; but none surrendered his integrity.

We do well to ponder the words of John Adams, who became our second president: "Posterity! You will never know how much it cost the present generation to preserve your freedom. I hope you will make good use of it. If you do not, I shall repent in heaven that I ever took half the pains to contend for it."

On Thanksgiving Day we declare our *dependence* upon God. We pause as a nation to say our annual thanks at the table of God's unending goodness. Thanksgiving is an amazing day because it is a day set aside not by the churches, but by our government; it falls right in the middle of the week when business is heating up for the Christmas rush; and the giving of thanks is the most spiritual of acts. On Thanksgiving Day we acknowledge God as the giver of all good gifts. We celebrate God's providence and his guidance. For Thanksgiving Day is utterly pointless if there is no one to thank. Thanksgiving—to whom? To God.

45

There has been no official state church in our nation; and we are glad for that. But as between reverence and irreverence, America has been squarely on the side of reverence. Our nation has recognized that democracy cannot survive without morality, and morality cannot survive without religion. America has been a free arena where the exercise of religion is encouraged, each person according to the dictates of his own conscience.

Ours is a young land; a number of us have been privileged to live through a third—and more—of our nation's history. My grandparents came to these shores empty-handed, and my sisters and I have fared better here than we could have done in any other land and in any other time in history. We still have a long, long way to go to achieve 100 percent brotherhood, but I have seen in my lifetime real progress in the war on racism. And there is still far too much poverty in the richest nation in history—but here again we have seen progress. When I was a boy, eighty percent of the American people were poor; today, eleven percent are below the poverty line. The life span of the average American has increased from 50 to 74½ years since the early years of this century.

Though all is not right with the American dream, many things are right; let's get on with the task and fulfill the dream, not destroy it. Were the youth of our land—who have been given so much—content with the failures or even the partial successes of previous generations, we would be disappointed. Let us rejoice over the creative discontent of our youth which impels them, in a lover's quarrel with America, to seek to reduce the gap between the American dream and the American reality. Is there not much truth in Emerson's declaration: "Our whole history appears like a last effort of providence on behalf of the human race"? Lincoln expresses the same thought in his brilliant phrase, "our almost chosen people."

Another American holiday, the last Monday in May, is known as Memorial Day, a day in the beauty of springtime in which we tenderly deck our graves and remember those who have passed through the body and gone on. It is a day which stresses our *interdependence*. Democracy means a free people working together; if need be, sacrificing together; eternally vigilant. Others have toiled and sacrificed and we receive the fruit of their labors. When the leaders of the infant nation were working on the Constitution, someone asked the veteran Franklin: "Will it be a monarchy or a republic?" He smiled and replied: "A republic—if you can keep it." On Memorial Day we remember the million young men who have gone up to the altar of freedom and poured out a libation of their heart's blood. And we remember other myriad millions who have lived nobly—most often in quiet, unobtrusive ways—to further the cause of human freedom.

Washington pointed out in his Farewell Address that for America's freedom to endure, three things would be required: education, religion, and public good faith—in other words, a people who know what is right and then, knowing what is right, are eager to do what is right, in a partnership of confidence, realizing that if we don't hang together, we shall all hang separately.

The words spoken by the martyred Lincoln over the dead at Gettysburg come to mind: "We here highly resolve that these dead shall not have died in vain." On this Memorial Day when we remember especially those who have paid a great price for the preservation of our freedom, let freedom of worship be interpreted as freedom *to* worship, not freedom *from* worship. Let us fill our churches in praise and confession, and then walk humbly with our God. Let freedom of speech and the press result in speaking up for truth and justice in a keen sense of public responsibility, not in spewing forth rivers of filth; let freedom of assembly be for learning, for inspiration—not for vandalism and destruction.

Real freedom is not the right to do what we please, but when we are pleased to do what is right. Only as each of us respects the rights of others can he enjoy freedom for himself. Only as just and wise laws are fully obeyed is freedom complete. In a world where anything goes, soon everything is gone. America's greatest enemies are those within, who would make of this land not the land of the free and the home of the brave, but rather the land of the spree and the home of the knave. When a person spurns the laws of God, he ends up as a slave of his own appetites and passions. Revolutions by those who deny God end up by simply enthroning a new set of tyrants. Without God, the American dream becomes a nightmare.

We cannot long enjoy the fruits of freedom if we do not keep strong and vital the roots of freedom; namely, faith in God. The rights of man inevitably perish unless they are rooted deep in the righteousness of God.

Democracy is a way of effecting change without violence. Democracy is caring for a person as a person; Christianity is caring for every person as one for whom Christ died. Freedom is, therefore, a spiritual quality.

Freedom is never free; it is the costliest thing in the world. And freedom is never paid for in a lump sum; new installments come due in each generation. All our nation can give a new generation is the possibility of freedom. Youth cannot inherit freedom any more than they can inherit virtue—or character.

Democracy was born out of a spiritual faith; and as Woodrow Wilson said: "America must be redeemed spiritually if she is to endure materially."

America is committing sins on a wholesale scale which no other nation in history has gotten by with. It is a time to read and ponder such passages as Proverbs 14:34: "Righteousness exalts a nation, but sin is a reproach to any people."

Memorial Day is a time to pause and remember. We often recite the poem, "In Flander's Fields" by John McCrae, on Memorial Day: "To you from falling hands we throw/The torch, be yours to hold it high;/If you break faith with us who die,/We shall not sleep. . . ."

Yes, we need to remember why our brave men died. Is our lifestyle worthy of their supreme sacrifice? That nation which forgets its past history loses its future; it is doomed to make the same mistakes over and over. And the deeper call is in the midst of our mad pleasure chasing and materialism to remember the God of our fathers. In Deut. 8:6–20 we are reminded that if we have come into this good land and have waxed fat and prosperous only to forget God, then it shall go ill for us. And let us remember Jesus Christ the true liberator; for only when Christ has set us free are we truly free (2 Tim. 2:8, John 8:32–36). Freedom is bondage to the best. True liberty is freedom to do the will of God. In Christ's service is perfect freedom.

Look at our greatest patriotic songs. They all throb with a

clear recognition of the might and mercy of the God of history, the Lord of the nations.

Our national anthem, "The Star-Spangled Banner," as we move past the accustomed first stanza, calls upon our "heaven-rescued land" to "praise the Power that hath made and preserved us a nation"—and to follow justice as we make this our motto: "In God is our trust."

The final stanza of "America" is all prayer:

> Our Father's God, to Thee,
> Author of liberty,
>    To Thee we sing:
> Long may our land be bright
> With freedom's holy light;
> Protect us by Thy might,
>    Great God, our King.

Each stanza of "America the Beautiful" concludes with a prayer:

> America, America,
> God shed His grace on thee,
> And crown thy good with brotherhood
> From sea to shining sea.
>
>         .     .     .
>
> America, America,
> God mend thine every flaw,
> Confirm thy soul in self-control,
> Thy liberty in law.
>
>         .     .     .
>
> America, America,
> May God thy gold refine,
> Till all success be nobleness,
> And every grace divine.

And this beautiful song, which many feel would be a far stronger national anthem than "The Star-Spangled Banner," ends with a shining vision of what our land, redeemed by God's grace, with her diverse people living in brotherhood, could be.

"The Battle Hymn of the Republic" is a hymn of the judgment and mercy of Christ, calling each of us, redeemed by him, to "die to make men free"—or, as increasing numbers are singing it also, to "*live* to make men free."

As human beings we are endowed with the twin gifts of the "backreach" of memory and the outreach of hope. On Memorial Day we can exercise both. We can draw strength and courage from yesterday; with memory, says Barrie, we can even have "roses in December." We can draw encouragement from tomorrow, too. America has always been long on hope. The immigrants endured untold hardships buoyed by this thought: "Tomorrow it will be better." America for them was "the land of the future." It still is. As Eisenhower said: "There is nothing wrong with America that the faith in God and the love of freedom and the energy and intelligence of her citizens cannot cure."

The poet (known only to God) voices some fundamental truths when he says:

> I know three things must ever be,
>   to keep a nation strong and free;
> One is a hearthstone bright and dear,
>   with busy, happy loved ones near;
> One is a ready heart and hand,
>   to love and serve and keep the land;
> One is a worn and beaten way
>   to where the people go to pray;
> So long as these are kept alive
>   nation and people will survive;
> God keep them always everywhere:
>   the *hearth*, the *flag*, the *place of prayer*.

It is said that a threefold cord is not easily broken. May we together weave three strong and essential strands of *independence* from human tyranny with *dependence* upon a holy and loving God and *interdependence* upon our own honest toil and unselfish service and that of our fellow Americans into an unbreakable cord.

# THERE IS A GLORY

*Arnold T. Olson*

*President, Evangelical Free Church of America,
Minneapolis, Minnesota*

Far be it from me to glory except in the cross of our Lord Jesus Christ.
Gal. 6:14

The flag of the United States was officially conceived by the Continental Congress almost a year after the Declaration of Independence. It was on June 14, 1777, that the Congress resolved that "the flag of the United States shall be thirteen stripes alternate red and white, with a union of thirteen white stars of white on blue field, representing a new constellation." However, the final number of stripes was not fixed at that time. Two more stripes were added in 1795 when Vermont and Kentucky were admitted to the Union. And so it remained until 1818 when the number of states had increased to twenty. It was then that the design was fixed to allow for a new star for each state in the Union and a return to the thirteen stripes representing the original thirteen colonies. The designation of June 14 as Flag Day was not made until 1914 and that in a declaration by President Woodrow Wilson.

No flag in the world has had more attention given it by poet, preacher, and politician. Controversies and conflicts have arisen over its use and misuse. Even the Supreme Court has been involved in decisions pertaining to its proper recognition.

On this Flag Day we will look at Old Glory and at ourselves, first from the viewpoint of patriotism, but beyond that in terms of our relationship as Christians to the glory of the flag in light of the glory of the cross of Christ. We will consider in turn the waving, the wearing, and the worshiping of the flag.

The idea of waving a flag appears often in the Scriptures, where the flag was given a variety of names—standard, ensign, banner. "Every man of the children of Israel shall pitch by his standard,

51

with the ensign of their father's house" (Num. 2:2), "... terrible as an army with banners" (Cant. 6:10), "His banner over me was love" (Cant. 2:4), "He will lift up an ensign to nations from afar" (Isa. 5:19), "Declare among the nations, and publish, and set up a standard ..." (Jer. 50:2).

May the day never come when we are ashamed to wave the standard, the banner, the ensign, the flag of our United States. We have much more of which to be proud than ashamed. We may complain about the rising crime rate and the growing disregard for law and order. We may be ashamed of the corruption in government and the moral decay in high places, but as someone has well said, "I am not willing to let Watergate wash away my heritage. I don't want my concern over what we have lost to blind me to what we have left."

To wave it proudly does not mean to wave it blindly. We are aware of the fact that "righteousness exalteth a nation: but sin is a reproach to any people" (Prov. 14:34). This truth is applicable to the United States as well as all nations. There are dark chapters in our history—the exploitation of the American Indian, the practice of slavery, the prejudices against minorities. In reading these chapters, we must not skip the many we can review with pride.

Paul E. Sherer writing in the magazine called *The Chaplain* back in 1944 said: "The flag stands for the devotion and sacrifice of those who have gone before me, loving their freedom, refusing to abuse it, laboring for it with clean conscience; putting their lives into it. It stands for justice. It stands for the equality of all men under God, whatever their color or creed. It stands for my voice and yours in the affairs of government, my human and my sacred duty."

It is easy to complain about what's wrong about America. It is easy to forget that to others, our country, with all her faults, is still the most desired land in the world. Let us think about what's good about America and wave the flag proudly. In so doing we apply the Scripture: "Whatever things are honest, Whatever things are just, Whatever things are pure, Whatever things are lovely, Whatever things are of good report; if there be any virtue, and if there be any praise, think on these things" (Phil. 4:8).

Wearing the flag in the lapel has become the "in thing" during recent years. For some it has become a symbol of hypocritical patriotism. The image of a president of the United States lying to his people while wearing the flag has tarnished the symbol. The wearing of the flag calls for self-examination—am I a worthy citizen of the country whose flag I wear?

Patriotism is more than flying the flag on June 14, waving it on July 4, or wearing it at a political rally. True patriotism involves more than an attitude to one's country. It includes the right spirit within. It was Martin Luther who wrote, "The prosperity of a country depends not on the abundance of the revenues, nor the beauty of its public buildings, nor the strength of its fortifications; but consists in the number of its cultivated citizens, its men of enlightenment, education, and character. Here are to be found its true interests, its chief strength, its real power."

The spectacle of leaders of our nation on trial in the very courts they once administered and sitting in prison is one of the great tragedies of this decade. Many of them wear the flag unworthily. But how about you? How about me? It takes a great people to produce great leaders. A great people will produce great men who can lead us to new ventures of faith and new exploits in national righteousness.

Congress has passed laws against the desecration of the flag as well as its proper use, size, and display. Is not the wearing of the flag unworthily also a form of desecration?

While the waving and the wearing of the flag have their place, the worshiping of the flag is always out of place for the Christian. There are limits to patriotism. A Christian must recognize a loyalty which rises above loyalty to a national flag. Old Glory must not replace the glory of the cross. There are times when one must carefully review the proper place of the flag in relation to the cross. The flag, in the church, is to be on the right of the speaker, not above the pulpit. In the Pledge of Allegiance to the flag of the United States of America we add that it is symbolic of the Republic and one nation *under God.* The Pledge of Allegiance to the flag is secondary to an allegiance to Jesus Christ. That is the highest form of patriotism. No great concept of democracy is safe until it is laid in the hands of God.

The early believers decided that there were occasions (such as upon being ordered to repress their Christian witness), when they would have to obey God rather than man. Dr. Halford E. Luccock, in a provoking article entitled "Pagan Emblems on Christian Altars," uses the flag as one example. While being careful not to rule the flag out of the church, nevertheless he states that it has often been a pagan emblem representing a nationalism which sets itself up in the place of God, claiming to be the supreme object of a citizen's devotion, the lord of his body and soul, the arbiter of his conscience. In a national crisis the cross is thus put under a moratorium.

We welcome naturalized citizens to our country. In fact, most of us are either naturalized citizens or their descendants. Might the time have come when we need to ask ourselves the question, Have I become a *neutralized* citizen? Was it not a nation of neutralized citizens that produced a Hitler?

Senator Mark Hatfield of Oregon, in a speech at Messiah College in 1973, put it succinctly:

> The more I observe contemporary America, and the more I read about the history of the church and the more I study the Scriptures, the more I sense how dangerous it is to merge our piety with patriotism. What I want to say is that the Christian, like every citizen, cannot avoid being political in some sense. What he must do is bring the political realm of his life under the authority of Jesus Christ. Our politics must never be ruled by thoughtless conformity to the culture in which we live. ... The Christian owes obedience as long as this does not involve disobedience to God. Whenever the State and God come into direct conflict, the Christian must obey God. The Christian should pray for the State and the authorities, regardless of how good or how bad, just or unjust they may be. Finally, the Christian must witness to the State by his words, and his acts. He must demonstrate that Christ is sovereign over all, that ultimately we are all bound to the law of love. The Bible gives us no basis for uncritically accepting the State, or for totally rejecting it either. Rather, the Bible tells us that at times Caesar and God may come into conflict and if they do, we must never render unto Caesar that which is rightfully God's.*

Was not this what President Woodrow Wilson had in mind when he established June 14 as National Flag Day: "Let us on

---

* Quoted from the *Evangelical Visitor*, official magazine of the Brethren in Christ Church, 10 August 1973. Used by permission.

that day rededicate ourselves to the nation, 'one and inseparable,' from which every thought that is unworthy of our forefathers first vow of independence, liberty, and right shall be excluded, and in which we shall stand with united hearts for all America which no man can corrupt, no influence draw away from its ideals, no force divide against itself, a nation signally distinguished among all nations of mankind for its clear, undivided conception alike of its duties and its privileges, its obligations and its rights."

Whatever failures may have been America's since the first Flag Day, may we make the dedication a true one so we can continue to wave the flag proudly, wear the flag worthily, but always keep the cross of Christ above the flag. Only then will Old Glory keep its beauty and inspire devotion to the one nation under God and the Republic for which it stands.

# WHAT IS A "NATION UNDER GOD"?

*Dean M. Kelley*

*Executive Director, Department of Civil and Religious Liberty, National Council of Churches, New York, New York*

In 1953, two new words were added to the Pledge of Allegiance to the flag. It now says, "...one nation *under God*, indivisible, with liberty and justice for all." The change makes the rhythm a bit awkward, but the addition seems to say something that is important to many people. Just what does it mean? How is a "nation under God" different from a nation *not* "under God"? And who adopted whom?

To say a nation is "under God" may mean one of several things.

If it means that the nation is under the governance and judgment of God, it is a statement of the obvious. *All* nations and persons are under the governance and judgment of God. But perhaps the important thing is that the nation officially *recognizes* or *affirms* that it is subordinated to a higher power. Is that what those words mean? It depends on which way they work.

Does it mean that this nation is uniquely and distinctively "under God" in some way that other nations are not? Is it a claim to some special relationship between the United States and God? That is the way many generations of Americans have understood the situation, beginning with the early settlers of New England, who believed that God had sent them as his "new Israel" on an "errand into the wilderness" to settle a new "promised land," to become a "city set upon a hill" as an example to all nations of what a Christian commonwealth should be.

As many peoples of differing persuasions came to these shores, it was gradually recognized that the civil commonwealth was no longer, if it ever was, a homogeneous believing religious community. And so a great institutional invention was developed:

For the first time in human history, the civil community was separated from, or made independent of, the religious community. Citizens no longer had to believe alike religiously in order to be members of the same civil community.

But some religious beliefs persisted in secular guise. The belief in being a "chosen people" survived in a phrase used by John O'Sullivan in the mid-nineteenth century to express the common confidence in national purpose: "Our manifest destiny [is] to overspread the continent allotted by Providence for the free development of our yearly multiplying millions." Under Teddy Roosevelt, the "manifest destiny" of the United States was expanded to encompass other parts of the world, to whom we would bring peace, democracy, enlightenment—whether they wanted it or not.

The effect of calling ourselves "a nation under God"—and of making In God We Trust the official motto of the nation—can be to claim the blessings of God for ourselves and our nation, whether other nations get any or not. It can be a way of asserting that God somehow endorses what we do—that "somebody up there likes us."

But God does not endorse the petty and imperfect systems of any nation or of all nations. God is not a "good American"; he is not an American at all! He is not more interested in America than in other nations. He has declared through the prophets what the true situation is:

"For my thoughts are not your thoughts, neither are my ways your ways, says the Lord" (Isa. 55:8). No people can put the Creator of the universe in their pocket; no nation can claim special favors from the Judge of *all* nations.

The only way in which a nation can claim to be "under God" in any special way that means anything is by making a thorough and continuous effort to obey his will. It is not a matter of insisting that "God is on our side," but of putting ourselves on *his* side. This demands a different sort of life from the one we may have been leading before we came "under God." If we are still the same old self-seeking, greedy, ruthless, envious, gluttonous, malicious animals we were before, then taking on the phrase "under

God" is indeed "taking the Lord's name in vain," the essence of profanity indulged in on a national scale.

One wonders whether the good Lord God *wants* us claiming to be "under" him if our deeds do not honor his will. It used to be, thousands of years ago, that human beings thought God was pleased with ceremonies of praise and rituals of homage to him, accompanied by incense and sacrifices. But eight hundred years before Christ, the Hebrew prophets introduced a radical, revolutionary notion: God was more concerned with how people treated each other! (Isa. 1:12–17; Mic. 6:8). And Jesus denounced those who give him lip service in place of heart service: "Why do you call me 'Lord, Lord', and not do what I tell you?" (Luke 6:46).

In view of this scriptural background, what would a *real* "nation under God" look like? A nation truly "under God" would not need to engrave In God We Trust on its coins or proclaim it as a national motto. Its trust in God would be apparent to all from its actions. Our actions proclaim that our trust is in almost everything but God! In Nuclear Weapons We Trust, and In Protective Tariffs We Trust, and In Immigration Restrictions We Trust, and In Security Investigations We Trust.

A nation truly "under God" might also be more careful about where it puts God's name. God's name on the coins and the currency does not sanctify commercial transactions so much as it trivializes the name of God. Is it not one of the clearest examples of using God's name "in vain"? Can you not hear Jesus saying to our time: "It is not the name on the coin that sanctifies it, but the motives of the men who buy and sell with it and the uses of the things that are bought and sold. Woe unto you, hypocrites and idolaters! that you write the name of God on money used to hire a prostitute or purchase a murder. Woe unto you, that you *say* In God We Trust while your deeds speak louder than your words that your trust is in everything else. *Show* by your deeds that your trust is in God, and you will not need to proclaim your virtue before the nations with hollow words."

A nation truly "under God" would not need to ask God's blessing at every session of courts, legislatures, and school assemblies.

(Not that these prayers are bad; they are simply a substitute for righteousness.) Such a nation would show its worthiness of God's blessing by its effective concern for the poor and the downtrodden. Segregation would be eliminated from all aspects of life, in the South and in the North. Decent homes would be accessible to all. Everyone would have a productive job in which to serve the needs of his neighbors and for which he would receive adequate pay. Demagogues would not be trying to stir up suspicion and hate and fear, turning neighbor against neighbor, but every citizen would try to live in peace and harmony and mutual respect with all others. Can you not hear Jesus saying to us: "Woe to you, hypocrites and idolaters! that you want your great men and your rulers to call often upon the name of God, and to offer prayers in the marketplace to be seen by men, but you do not require that they seek his will and do it, and you do not do so yourselves. Do not call upon God to bless the nation until you are prepared to do his will. Then indeed he will bless the nation without your needing to ask."

A nation truly "under God" would not need to prove its piety by providing chapels and chaplains at public expense in prisons and hospitals. Chapels and chaplains are not bad; they may provide comfort and consolation to many who are caught in a strange and hostile institutional environment. But they can be a substitute for the more direct ministry of healing and recovering which these institutions can and should perform.

It is a credit to the spirit of Christ that hospitals exist. They have been nobly conceived and constructed to alleviate suffering and cure disease. They render the most direct and devoted service to man and to God by their healing function. But the nation has grown weary in well-doing and has ceased to provide adequately for its hospitals. Their equipment deteriorates and their walls crumble. Even public hospitals rely upon volunteers for many basic services and repairs and expect their poorest paid employees to subsidize the care of the sick, even buying soap for the patients out of their meager wages! Can you not hear Jesus saying to us: "Woe to you, hypocrites and idolaters! that you pretend to care for your neighbor, by providing buildings in which the sick and the suffering can be confined, but once they are within, you do not care what becomes of them. You neither minister unto them yourselves, nor provide wherewithal for others to do so; yet you send a priest in to them to pray in their midst, saying, 'Behold, we are a nation under God, for we will not imprison a man without Scripture, nor execute him without prayer!' "

A nation truly "under God" would not need to post the Ten Commandments like No Smoking signs in the classrooms, nor distribute free Bibles to schoolchildren. There are already more Bibles around than are ever read. When more than half the adult population (according to a recent survey) cannot name *one* of the first four books of the New Testament, it is a little premature for us to claim to be a nation "under God."

It would be plainer and more persuasive for children to find the Ten Commandments written on the hearts of their elders and visible in all their actions, so that the younger generation would grow up knowing no other example but righteousness. But instead, what do they find? They find thieves in high places, stealing from the public treasury or from those who have trusted them with honor and responsibility. They find corruption throughout adult life—from "respectable" or white-collar crime to chiseling on a grand scale in payola, price fixing by corporations, bribery of inspectors by contractors in the building of schools, and all manner of graft, kickbacks, fee splitting, extortion, embezzlement—casually accepted and expected by everyone without a sign of moral indignation. Compared to these rackets *juvenile* delinquency is mild indiscretion. And the very people who participate in this corruption have the smug and hypocritical gall to claim that they are a "nation under God"! Repeating the Ten Commandments ten times a day will not overcome the effect of that example! Can you not hear Jesus saying to us: "Woe to you, hypocrites and idolaters! for you are like whitewashed tombs, which outwardly appear beautiful, but within are full of dead men's bones and all uncleanness. You teach children the Ten Commandments, but you do not obey them yourselves. First show by your lives that you consider God's law important, and then your children will follow you."

A nation truly "under God" would spend more than a penny of every dollar of family income for religion and charity. When tobacco, liquor, cosmetics, amusements *each* attract far greater expenditures every year than religion and charity combined, it is simply ridiculous, if not blasphemous, for us to claim to be a nation *under God*! More realistic would be the claim that we are a nation "under the influence of alcohol," devoted to recessed filters and pancake makeup. Let's leave God out of it until we can give him something more solid than idle boasting. Can you not hear Jesus saying: "Verily, this nation honors me with their lips, but their hearts are far from me!"

The only way our nation will ever be "under God" in any Christian sense is through the repentance, redemption, and devotion of its citizens. Without this renewal of its moral fiber and fervor, our nation will gradually subside into the slack and self-satisfied ruin that has befallen every great nation in its prosperity—regardless of whose name we put on the coins or pronounce when we salute the flag!

Each one of us can contribute to the strengthening of the nation, or to its further weakening. You can do it through the renewal of the spiritual strength and purity of one person—the only person *you* can change and for whom *you* are responsible—*yourself.* That is where the regeneration of America begins: with *me*, with *you.* Let it begin today!

# A DECLARATION OF DEPENDENCE

*R. H. Edwin Espy*

*Chairman, Project Forward '76;*
*Former General Secretary, National Council of Churches*

When, in the throes of divisive events, with friend estranged from friend on issues of national policy, it becomes necessary for all our people to strengthen the social bonds which have connected them with one another, and to affirm the cohesive and equal station to which the laws of nature and nature's God entitle us, a decent respect to the needs of our country requires that we should declare the causes that bind us together. A time of division is a time to affirm the grounds of our unity.

We are bound to all the people of the world by our common humanity as children of God. We are united as American citizens in devotion and responsibility under God to the nation in which we live. We have a further common bond as Americans of religious faith who seek a spiritual kingdom. We worship the God of the ages. The ground of our very being, the Creator of the universe, is the ultimate source of our unity. Our origin and faith in God far transcend our differences; we are one despite our diversity.

We remind ourselves and all Americans of our religious heritage as a nation. From our belief in God has sprung our devotion to liberty. At our best we have been a beacon and a haven to peoples from all the world, a sanctuary of freedom. And now in the twentieth century, when ideological indoctrination has subverted the minds and souls of millions, we still stand firm for religious and intellectual freedom. The free exercise of religion has been

[The Bicentennial Consultation on Religion and the American Experience held in Washington, D.C. May 21 -22, 1975, brought together some two hundred participants from the broadest religious spectrum ever assembled in America. This "Declaration," written by the former General Secretary of the National Council of Churches, which is adapted in part from portions of the Declaration of Independence, reflects the mood of that Consultation as to the role of religion in the life of our nation.]

and is the quintessence of all our freedoms, and our organized religious communities have nobly shared in America's struggle for liberty and justice for all.

But we as a nation, and those of us who call ourselves believers, have faltered grievously in our covenant with one another and with our God. Even when we have professed our faith we often have failed to practice it. Our treatment of many of our citizens, especially native Americans and other minorities, women, the aging, young people, and other less obvious segments of our society, has sometimes ranged us on the side of inhumanity. Our history on the whole has been lighted by liberty, but it has also been blighted by bigotry and exploitation.

We, therefore, in consultation and prayer assembled, appealing to the Supreme Judge of the nation and the world in the rectitude of our intentions, do first of all give thanks to God for his guidance, protection, advancement, and correction of our country. But we humbly acknowledge the injustices of which our people are guilty, in the past and in the present. We confess our complicity in our country's sins. We love our land and believe that, together with others, it has an honored place in the divine intention for humankind. We pray that the God of all peoples will help us to make of America a nation of peace and freedom and love and justice for all, both within our borders and in all the world.

We praise and honor our forebears for the political independence which they won for our nation. But we are now in an era of new human struggles around issues scarcely thought of two hundred years ago. We are faced with wanton violence, threats to the life of the family as we have known it, radical reassessments of moral and cultural values, new international responsibilities, economic perplexities, a pace of social change so rapid and drastic that we seem unable to assess or direct it.

With the people of our country in disarray over what is right and what is wrong, our foremost need is internal. We hold honest differences of opinion, but we also yield to unreasoned strife. We fall victim to crime on the one hand and suppression on the other, and often the two are interlocked.

Our nation is strong, and we are confident that we can surmount these difficulties with the help of the Almighty, but only in reliance upon him. We are called to rekindle the flame of human liberty, lighting it with the torch of religious freedom with which God has blessed America. Only on the basis of liberty can we have a society of justice. Only so can we face our differences openly and together and transform our divisions into unity.

Our need, therefore, at the threshold of our third century is not to redeclare our independence but to build responsible interdependence, both among our own people and between our people and the other peoples of the world. For both national independence and human interdependence we must commit our wills to the will of God, in whom all humanity is one. The only sure foundation for human community is the divine order, the eternal verities and values of the Creator of the universe.

We therefore declare our dependence upon Almighty God. It was the Author of liberty who inspired our independence. The Source of all being is the ground of our interdependence. We reaffirm with the framers of the Declaration of Independence our firm reliance on the protection of Divine Providence. God is our help in ages past, our hope for years to come.

To the Lord of all life be honor and glory, and to us may the grace of the divine love and truth and peace and freedom and justice be ever present. May God's will be done in the United States of America and in all the world.

# PUTTING LABOR IN ITS PLACE

*Leighton Ford*

*Evangelist, Billy Graham Evangelistic Association, Charlotte, North Carolina*

Throughout North America the traditional Labor Day weekend is being observed. In a way it is ironic that we *honor* labor by having a day when we do *no* labor!

Most men and women still prefer to belong to a hive of workers —not a nest of drones. Two University of Michigan researchers asked a large sampling of workers if they would continue to work even if they had enough money to live comfortably without work. Eighty percent of the workers surveyed replied that they would want to work even if a large windfall put them on easy street.

That commitment to work should not surprise us, for work is a basic element in our human makeup. Archaeologists have noted how frequently primitive tools are found near the remains of our human ancestors. And someone has suggested that the familiar term, *Homo sapiens*, which means "man, the thinker," should probably be *Homo faber*, "man the worker."

Many of our surnames are actually descriptions of types of work. Heading the list is Smith, and the village smithy has pages of descendants listed in any phonebook. Countless other names describe occupations: Taylor, Cook, Baker, Hunter, Butcher, Farmer, and many, many more.

Have you noticed that when two people are first introduced, the question, How do you do? is often followed by another: *What* do you do?

Elliott Jacques, an industrial social scientist, has stated, "Work does not satisfy [man's] material needs alone. In a very deep sense it gives him a measure of his sanity." At the very beginning of creation God gave man the mandate to work: "Be fruitful and multiply and fill the earth and subdue it," the Lord commanded

(Gen. 1:28). God has ordained work for our own good and that of society.

Some societies have belittled work as the function of slaves. But Christianity honors work! Jesus our Lord labored as a carpenter (Mark 6:3). His first disciples were fishermen, and there is no word of apology for their status as workers. Even the intellectual Apostle Paul worked at his trade as a tentmaker (Acts 18:3), and set as an economic rule that "if any will not work, neither shall he eat" (2 Thess. 3:10). The other side of the coin, said Jesus, is that "the laborer is worthy of his hire" (Luke 10:7).

That much maligned "Protestant work ethic," correctly understood, is a biblical work ethic. It is not a threatening club. It is a divinely ordered prescription for our well-being. We sometimes joke about our work and about getting back to the daily grind or the salt mines. Seriously, however, we should thank God for the opportunity to work.

It's obvious that for millions of people work has become a burden rather than a blessing. The best selling book, *Working*, by Studs Terkel includes interviews with many ordinary people who are fed up with their work. It is not just that people need more pay to keep up with inflation, but much work has become boring and meaningless. Many studies blame on-the-job boredom for the increase in violence.

Part of the reason is the repetitious nature of the assembly line, where the worker is only a kind of machine going through the motions. But the deeper truth is that the entrance of sin changed work from a joy into a toil! God told Adam after he had sinned: "Cursed is the ground because of you ... in toil you shall eat of it ... in the sweat of your face shall you eat bread" (Gen. 3:17–19). Because of sin, work has lost its true value. It has become an end in itself, and often the means of exploitation and oppression.

Yet Jesus Christ redeems work! We are not saved by our works, secular or religious, but by the grace of God received by faith (Eph. 2:8–10). But when we receive Christ we also gain a new perspective on work. The Christian can see the most menial chore as an opportunity to bring glory to the One who has saved him from his sins and placed him in the family of God. He understands what the Apostle Paul meant when he urged: "Whatever you do or say, let it be as a representative of the Lord Jesus. . . ." (Col. 3:17). That "whatever you do" includes your job—yes, that humdrum job—not glamorous perhaps, but the arena in which God can be glorified in your experience.

Above his laboratory door George Washington Carver had a descriptive sign. It read: God's Little Workshop. Is it any wonder that from that humble laboratory came a stream of innovative discoveries that transformed the face of rural America? Dr. Carver felt that he glorified God as he experimented and discovered new uses for the humble peanut.

You and I glorify God in our work—first of all, by being the best workers possible. No one is impressed with the testimony of a professing Christian who is a shoddy worker or a shirker on the work team. God deserves only our best on the assembly line, in the office, the classroom, the department store, the hospital laboratory, or wherever we work. Actually we earn the right to testify by word when we demonstrate a competence and sense of responsibility at our place of work.

After all, a large portion of life is spent at our place of employment. A twenty-one-year-old facing a life of work with retirement at sixty-five has ahead of him eighty-eight thousand hours of employment. That is a major share of life and, if we cannot glorify God in some way during those hours, our impact for God is nullified for a major part of our earthly existence.

Probably someone wonders how he could possibly count for God in the minor position which is his lot in life. Writing to slaves who were members of the church at Colossae, the Apostle Paul counseled: "Work hard and cheerfully at all you do, just as though you were working for the Lord and not merely for your masters" (Col. 3:23). Those Christian slaves had discovered the secret of emancipated living that was unknown to their non-Christian masters. If slaves could glorify God in that cruel, repressive society, surely Christian workers in the Western world can make their place of service to be a temple of praise.

This does not mean, of course, that Christian employers are to be slave masters. The Christian businessman should recognize that many of the jobs in our modern society are dull, tedious, and unfulfilling. He should do everything possible to help his employees break out of the rut of uncreative, dead-end jobs and see their work as part of a whole creative service enterprise.

On this Labor Day weekend I challenge you to demonstrate your Christian commitment in the place of work where God has placed you.

Young people today have charged that many adults are so job oriented that they have lost the joy of living. Instead of dismissing that charge offhand, I think we should pause to consider its validity. Do we not have to concede that a job, like anything else, can loom too large in our lives?

A word has been coined to describe someone in that state. He is a "workaholic"—one who is addicted to his work just as an alcoholic is addicted to liquor. His every waking hour is taken up with his work, and he has little or no time for anyone or anything else. We condemn the narcotic addict or the alcoholic, but our work-oriented society heaps honors upon the workaholic.

Dr. Nelson Bradley, chief of psychiatric studies at Lutheran General Hospital in Chicago, warns that "the person who is a work addict is rushing us to the grave. Our unquestioning acceptance of him is frightening; by his compulsive work habits, he has toiled his way into a position of power, and now he holds our fate in his hands."

Work addiction is a case of something good getting out of hand to become a monster. The all-consuming absorption with work elbows out other beautiful things and natural relationships. The workaholic's wife suffers, his family suffers, and he himself suffers —as does any addict. Work, which is God's provision for man's well-being, becomes to the workaholic a source of poison.

Someone has proposed a practical system of priorities to avoid the tyranny of work. The scale consists of four words: First, be a *person*; then, a *partner*; next, a *parent*; and finally, a *producer*.

First, be a real *person*—a fulfilled human being who has become a new creature in Jesus Christ and who is developing toward spiritual maturity.

Then, be a *partner*. When you marry someone, you become one flesh. If work interferes and disrupts that relationship, then work is as much an enemy as heroin would be.

Next, be a *parent*. Your children are uniquely yours—God's gift to you. Don't permit addiction to work to cause you to lose them or scar their lives.

Then, the final priority is your profession or work. By all means, as I have pointed out, be the best possible *producer*. But you will bring your best to your work when you are the master of your job, not your job the master of you. In this matter the word of God counsels a healthy, balanced outlook—honest work to the glory of God, not work as the ruthless dictator of your destiny.

Such an ideal can be a reality only if Jesus Christ is at the center of your life. When he is on the throne of your life, other people and priorities more readily find their slot. But first you must turn your life over to him by a personal act of faith. Right now, where you are, you can admit your sin and need and trust him as your Savior and Lord.

His call this Labor Day is unchanged: "Come to me and I will give you rest...all of you who work so hard beneath a heavy yoke" (Matt. 11:28).

# FROM LABOR DAY TO LEISURE DAY

*Robert Lee*

*Professor of Social Ethics, San Francisco Theological Seminary and Graduate Theological Union, San Francisco, California*

Come to me, all who labor and are heavy-laden, and I will give you rest.
                                                    Matt. 11:28

Special days are remembered in special ways.  The tradition of the Middle Ages was to observe special events (Saints' days) with celebration and festivity.  How are we to observe Labor Day in present day America?  I suggest that we consider the spirit of rest, which is an aspect of the ethics of leisure.  For rest puts us in touch with the wellsprings of our creativity and reminds us of who we are as creatures of the Almighty.

About a century ago, an eminent Scottish literary figure, Thomas Carlyle, proclaimed the "gospel of work."  As one might expect, this gospel fell on receptive ears, for Western industrial civilization was advancing by leaps and bounds.  As workers put shoulder to plow, they had their efforts blessed by the sanctity of Christian faith and ethics.

Today the gospel of work is incomplete without a "gospel of leisure."  When the workweek has declined from seventy hours one hundred years ago to forty or less today, when life expectancy has shifted from forty to seventy years or more, when the average American worker today has over twelve hundred more hours per year or one hundred more hours per month to spend on nonjob-related activities, as compared with his grandfather at the turn of the century, then I say it is high time to forge a leisure ethics.

Unlike the gospel of work, a new leisure ethics is not easy for Americans to accept.  It may well fall on deaf ears.  We have declared Labor Day as a national holiday.  But who has ever heard of setting aside a "Leisure Day?"  The average person in

70

the pew is a workaholic who has not only imbibed well the traditional work ethic, but is drunk and driven by its demons. People addicted to the work ethic have their entire life defined by their work. Such people, who have no reason for living apart from their work, are prone to psychogenic diseases, especially on weekends, holidays, and vacations. They suffer from acute leisureitis.

A spectacularly wide range of choices even now confronts the leisure tastes of most Americans. In the future we will be invited to choose on an even broader plane. Leisure will bring unprecedented opportunities for exercising freedom, for persons to become more fully human. At the same time, many individuals will seek to escape from this awesome and terrifying burden of freedom; they may drift with chance or circumstance and lapse into inhumanity instead of realizing their full human potential.

Let us cite a concrete example of what the future may hold for women, some of whom now feel burdened with household or menial chores. We know that with labor saving devices not only in factory and office, but also in the home, many American housewives are bored stiff and feel their talents are being wasted. They long for a fuller, more meaningful, and abundant life. More and more women will seek for satisfaction through a career or a part-time job that they can combine with their household duties. Even now a few creative women in our society feel burdened with the prospects of a nine months' pregnancy, which, so to speak, puts them out of commission. In the future, for those who want to exercise their freedom, they may well have the option of eliminating the nine months' pregnancy, culminated by "labor." We may expect to see fetal deliveries after one month, so that a creative working mother who wants to, can deliver after one month and return to the hospital to pick up her child after nine months!

Even more miraculous (and we don't really expect miracles anymore from science, for today's miracle has a way of becoming tomorrow's reality), don't be surprised to find a sleep machine in the future—an "electrosone" that is capable of packing a full night's deep, restful sleep into just two hours. Such a machine is now being tested. Imagine the revolutionary implications for leisure time once this device is perfected!

We must not forget the future implications that the leisure revolution will have for those currently unemployed. First, I regard it as a matter of *when* not *whether or not* we will see the guaranteed annual income become part of our national way of life. Barely whispered a few years ago and exposed to charges of un-Americanism, the idea is gaining ground, and I suspect will become firmly rooted a decade hence.

Implicit in the discussions about unemployment is the broader question about the meaning of work. One frequently hears it said that we will no longer need to work in the future. This misses the point. What we are confronted with is that the traditional meaning of work as being something productive, that one produces by dint of hard labor, muscles, and sweat—this kind of work will be consigned precisely where it belongs, that is, to the machine (the machine being to modern man what slaves were to the Greeks). And then man can turn his attention more to human pursuits. Leisure opportunities mean that man may turn to the art of living, and not be confined merely to the business of making a living.

There is much work now that needs doing, and there will be more in the future—if we can shift our focus from the private sector to the public sector. Even now, perhaps 750 thousand people can be put to good and creative tasks in the endeavors of the public sector—teacher's aides, hospital workers, remedial education, housing. In our slum communities, we have "natural" community leaders who could work with clubs and gangs, who could be employed to channel and redirect pent-up energies. In a saner future, when we the people become more willing to spend public funds for the public good, when we realize the good that would result if we spent on human beings a fraction of what it now costs to put a man into space or to fight a war, then we will be willing to commit our resources to serving the public interest, while at the same time cutting down on unemployment.

In this same line, the future should see great strides taken in the creative arts, in the aesthetic dimensions of our existence. We have a culture of poverty and we also have a poverty of culture. One is struck in visiting European centers with what a vast amount of the public treasury is spent and what a large labor force must be employed to keep up the museums and parks and gardens which pepper each city's landscape. We have begun to appropriate sums for national parks and the preservation of natural areas. Again, the future will see vast hordes of visitors to these places. Indeed, the lovely grove of ancient redwoods in Muir Woods, California, an area which has stood in virginal beauty for perhaps thousands of years, is just now under the threat of extinction because so many visitors in recent years have been trampling through and disturbing the roots and perhaps upsetting nature's delicate balance.

Through all these future changes which are even now breaking into the present, we would do well to heed the good news of Jesus, "Come to me, all who labor and are heavy-laden, and I will give you rest."

Recall that in the Genesis account of creation God rested on the seventh day and beheld that "the work he had made was very good." This suggests that life's fulfillment is not to be identified completely with work, but that rest is an indispensable ingredient in the rhythm of work and rest and worship. Man's work, like his creator's, is crowned with his rest, and his chief end is not to labor but to enjoy and glorify God.

When viewed as a day of rest, Labor Day invites us to stop and appraise, to evaluate the totality of our lives, to examine its quality. Such self-scrutiny should lead to growth in self-understanding and self-awareness. In our self-understanding we gain spiritual self-affirmation—the courage to be ourselves: alive, vital, growing, and creative creatures.

Rest is the ability to wait upon the Lord. "They that wait upon the Lord shall renew their strength; . . . they shall run, and not be weary" (Isa. 40:31). To rest is to recreate. Dennis de Rougemont has suggested that the verb "to create" is so powerful and precious that it should be reserved only for God. As creatures of God, we are not creators, but we are recreators. To recreate means to use whatever talent, resourcefulness, imagination, and capacity for appreciation one has at one's disposal for the sake of inner satisfaction and growth. Recreation may involve restoration —the resting and recharging of tired muscles, frayed nerves, and overworked brain cells.

Above all, man's creative activity relates him to the Creator of all things. Recreation is rest in God. We may rest from our labors, but we rest upon God, and we are strengthened in our dependence upon God.

Rest means the fullness of joy in God's works, so that our own work is not taken with ultimate seriousness. It is not the be-all and end-all of life. Perhaps this is what Jesus is saying to us in the account of Martha and Mary. Recall that Jesus rebukes Martha—the one who waits diligently upon him with service and becomes angry with her sister for waiting upon the Lord merely by listening to his teaching. "Lord," exclaims Martha, "Do you not care that my sister has left me to serve alone? Tell her then to help me." But Jesus answered her, "Martha, Martha, you are *anxious and troubled about many things*; one thing is needful. Mary has chosen the good portion, which shall not be taken away from her" (Luke 10:40–42).

May this Labor Day be a Leisure Day opportunity for you. May you find rest from your labors, refreshment from your toilsome ways, new and deeper and richer insights concerning yourself; may you see the neighbor and his relation to you, and may you learn to serve your neighbor. Then in this service, may you find God and his glory, and may you join with your neighbors in praise of him, from whom comes our labor and our leisure and, indeed, every good and perfect gift.

# PIETY AND PATRIOTISM:
# THE DILEMMA OF THE CHRISTIAN CITIZEN

*Lee E. Snook*

*Associate Professor, Systematic Theology,*
*Luther Theological Seminary,*
*St. Paul, Minnesota*

And he came to Nazareth, where he had been brought up; and he went to the synagogue, as his custom was, on the sabbath day. And he stood up to read; and there was given to him the book of the prophet Isaiah. He opened the book and found the place where it was written,

> "The Spirit of the Lord is upon me,
> because he has anointed me to preach good news to the poor.
> He has sent me to proclaim release to the captives
> and recovering of sight to the blind,
> to set at liberty those who are oppressed,
> to proclaim the acceptable year of the Lord."
>
> Luke 4:16–19

Let every person be subject to the governing authorities. For there is no authority except from God, and those that exist have been instituted by God.
Rom. 13:1

But our commonwealth is in heaven, and from it we await a Savior, the Lord Jesus Christ. . . .
Phil. 3:20

As a campus pastor during the decade of the sixties, I saw it happen again and again. I particularly remember seeing it happen with Richard. I emphasize the "remember" because his generation seems to be very much part of the past. Richard came east to the university from a midwest city and from a very pious Christian family. He himself exhibited all the virtues which one associates with middle America and with Christian piety, and he did so in a very attractive manner. He quickly became active in the religious community at the university, was a serious student, a leader in one

75

of the political clubs, and a staff member of the daily campus newspaper. His columns often defended the policies of the government at a school where such opinions were not only rare, but popularly scorned.

One summer Richard spent his vacation as a student volunteer working in a village in South Vietnam. In the fall he returned to school very much transformed. He seemed to withdraw from many of his previous interests. Most of his youthful ideals about God and country were badly shaken, replaced by near bitterness. He sensed that he had been deceived by beliefs about his country, beliefs which were contradicted by his own experiences and observations. Richard would probably never again assume that there is a simple connection between Christian piety and American patriotism.

In recent years many Christian congregations, indeed many Christian families, have undergone internal conflicts because of personal disagreements about what it means to be both a Christian and a citizen. This has often been a vexing question in the history of Christianity, but in a period when American politics have such worldwide effects, it is all the more important for American Christians to face squarely the implications of their faith for their citizenship in a nation whose government is of the people, for the people, and by the people, and whose government has a profound influence upon the lives of all the people of God's created earth.

Especially for a discussion of this troubling issue, the Scriptures must be the foundation and ought to provide the important boundaries. The Scriptures, in fact, were the basic source of guidance for many who came to this continent from Europe. The first settlers often looked to the Bible to find ways to express what they were about. America, for some of them, was to be the New Israel, a city set upon a hill, the city of God, the wilderness from which they could wrest a new Garden of Eden. They thought of themselves as partners with God in a new covenant, and they trusted themselves to the providence of God for their future.

Surely Christians today can scarcely do less than turn to Scripture as the primary source of guidance for their own citizenship in America, regardless of how greatly America has changed from the days when Europeans on this continent regarded themselves as chosen by God for a new political venture. Even if American Christians today cannot easily think of themselves as God's chosen people, they can still look in faith to Scripture.

We cannot assume, however, that what was the word of God for them is still the word of God for us in the same way. Our situation is no longer parallel either to the Israelites or to the New England settlers. Some who came to this land could claim those passages of Scripture as God's word to them because they were, in fact, vulnerable, poor, dispossessed, and unable to return to the land from which they had fled.

God favors the poor; but we are not a poor nation. And therefore we cannot claim the promises of God in Scripture in the same way as those who settled this land. We *can* claim God's promises, but not in the same way. Instead, we have to ask a different question, namely, What is God's word for us as a privileged, rich, powerful, and prosperous nation?

When we read Scripture in light of our own prosperity as a nation, we will notice certain things. First of all, because God does favor the poor, the laws of the Old Testament especially focus on the obligation to help the poor. And, of course, it is not only the Old Testament laws which safeguard the poor and which call upon the privileged to protect them, but the writings of the prophets also underscore again and again the rights of the poor.

The ministry of Jesus also reaffirmed in unambiguous terms the fact that God favors the poor, that God's judgment is against those who abuse the poor, and that God calls upon all who believe in him to serve him by serving the needs of "the least of these."

The Bible gives no room for doubt about God's concern for the poor, the dispossessed, the vulnerable, and the oppressed. By implication, God's judgment is against those who exploit the poor and who use their wealth and power in ways which render the poor even more wretched, either by neglect or by concentrating more and more wealth into the hands of fewer and fewer corporations or nations.

America is a rich nation. Many of its citizens are Christians. Its government is the government of the citizens and for the citi-

zens.  When Christian citizens consider their citizenship in a rich
and privileged nation, they cannot and ought not separate their
religious faith from their political responsibility.  While the Bible
is clear enough about God's commandment to those who are privileged, it is not at all clear as to what form the Christian's citizenship should take in a privileged nation like the United States of
America.

It is easier to see the relationship between piety and politics for
the New England Puritans than it is to see the same relationship
for American Christians in our day.  In the early 1600s, before
they left ship and set foot on American soil, the first settlers heard
a sermon from their leader, John Winthrop.  "We are entered," he
said, "into covenant with God for this work. . . ."

The relationship between piety and citizenship is not so clear for
us today.  The covenant made by the colonists was broken even as
it was made because the new commonwealth was itself founded
upon some very exclusivistic and intolerant principles inasmuch as
it permitted the bondage and destruction of other races.  Nevertheless, the failure of the covenant makers to keep the promise
ought not conceal from us the valid principle which remains,
namely, the fact that no social cohesion or human cooperation is
possible unless there is a shared commitment to that which, or to
the One Who, transcends all personal and local considerations.

We turn now to the broader and more immediate question of
how Christians can exercise their citizenship in ways that will be
faithful to Scripture on the one hand, and realistic about the complexities of American life on the other.

Our nation is rich and powerful, but it is not in any official sense
a Christian nation.  America is influential in the world, but it is
also troubled internally.  Many people in the world love and admire the United States, but we are also disliked and feared because
of the disproportion of resources which we consume in order to
maintain our prosperity.  Our nation is a model of freedom and
justice for many, but discrimination against minorities among our
citizens is well known around the world.  Many of our cities are in
serious difficulty.  Health care is not available equally to all our
citizens.  Crime is only one of the major symptoms of social un-

rest in this great and prosperous nation. Social unrest, in fact, is not only dangerous to the political health of our country, but is also a threat to the well-being of our religious communities.

Can we bring together these several factors, as far-reaching and complicated as they may be, and propose some principles which could guide us as we try to be both faithful Christians and responsible citizens? I believe there are at least three clear and down-to-earth principles upon which we could agree.

Christians have two citizenships, not merely one. Paul wrote to the Philippians, "Our commonwealth is in heaven." The Greek word for commonwealth is from the same root as the word for politics. Our commonwealth, our citizenship, our political loyalty is in heaven. Christians live in a community, a commonwealth, which is distinct from the many political structures of the world. Christians live in Christ. And that shared life in Christ can only be described with the language of spirit, of faith, and of a life-style consistent with that faith. But Paul also wrote to the Romans and said, "Let every person be subject to the governing authorities." Our heavenly citizenship does not cancel our citizenship in human governments. Some people will express and acknowledge loyalty to one government only. Christians can share that loyalty but it will not be the Christian's only loyalty. Jesus said, "Render to Caesar the things that are Caesar's and to God the things that are God's." He may not have specified which things are which, but Christians will believe that while some things belong to Caesar, not everything is owed to Caesar.

Even though Christians have two citizenships—the one a national citizenship and the other a citizenship which transcends nationalities—they live out or express their dual citizenship in one world, in the one world which God creates and sustains. In actual practice Christians have often confused their two citizenships and have wrongly expected the national government to deliver for them what can come only from faith in Christ, or Christians have expected their loyalty to Christ to deliver for them what is only appropriate for the human institution of government. When we wrongly expect salvation from our national citizenship, we are in danger of fanatical patriotism or dictatorships; when we expect our faith in Christ to bring us, somehow, automatic social tranquillity, we are in danger of an unrealistic and non-Christian otherworldliness, a pie-in-the-sky religion. Only if we are careful in distinguishing what is proper for each citizenship, will we likely avoid expecting the wrong thing from the two citizenships which are part of our Christian life in God's one created world.

Our third principle flows from the second. It is because Christians have two citizenships and try always to distinguish without separating the two that they ought also to refrain from expecting from one commonwealth what can only be delivered by the other. The principle here is that Christians do not expect America to be a specifically Christian community. The institutions of government such as the courts, the presidency, the Congress, the schools, or the law enforcement agencies are not the instruments by which God saves souls. Instead they are the means by which evildoers are restrained and proper human needs are served and advanced. Much of the mischief done by Christians as they have engaged in public life is the result of their trying to turn these instruments of government into tools for denominational ambitions.

On the other hand, it is just as mischievous for Christians to withdraw totally from public affairs, pretending that by so doing they are preserving Christianity from corruption. Christians should know, from Scripture at least, that God desires justice, favors the poor, judges those who misuse power and wealth, and calls upon those who believe in him to effect his will in public life. In public life God wills that there be justice. The instrument God uses for that work is the commonwealth of human government. God also desires that all persons be reconciled to him. The instrument he uses for that purpose is the church's ministry of the gospel of Jesus Christ.

It is very difficult for modern people to affirm that God works through the human institutions of government in order to bring about the justice which he wills for all humankind. Christians will usually affirm that God works through the gospel ministry of the church to save souls but, like many contemporary people, Christians are often skeptical about the notion that God is at work in the world of politics, government, or international affairs. Paul could affirm that governmental authorities are ordained by God—although of course he knew they often defy God's appointed role for them and become demonic. Early American settlers believed that God in his providence would ratify a just government in this new land. This principle is still valid, but is hard for many people to believe today not only because of dominant views of history, science, and psychology, but also because governments have so recently been exposed as corrupt. The doctrine of divine providence—prominent in Scripture and in the history of our own country—is a doctrine which ought to be high on the agenda of Christian reflection in this our nation's third century. Our ability to believe in God's providential working through our own efforts to be responsible citizens has been sorely tested.

There are reasons to hope that this necessary doctrine of divine providence, that is, of God at work in the human struggle for a just and peaceful society, will yet be sustained. One such reason is that people still worship in this land. It is just as well that our American belief in divine providence has been challenged, because we have tended to use that belief to justify some questionable American policies. Now that Americans have tasted failure overseas and sharp criticisms at home, we may be able to recover the meaning of some of the language we have been using in our worship all these years. God is at work in human affairs—but not always as we might wish. Perhaps our piety, nurtured in worship, has been wiser than our patriotism, encouraged by recent wars. A worshiping people might be better able to sustain a belief in the providence of God so necessary for a tranquil society, but it is not a blind belief. Instead it is a belief that God works where that which he wills for humankind is actively, politically, sought by human beings. Worshiping people are not as likely to neglect Divine Providence when, week after week, they remember the stories and prophecies of Scripture and when they sing:

> Wherever goodness lurks
> We catch thy tones appealing;
> Where man for justice works
> Thou art thyself revealing.

# THE ADMIRABLE ADMIRAL

*Francis J. Lally*

*Secretary, Department of Social Development and World Peace, U.S. Catholic Conference, Washington, D.C.*

When we think of Christopher Columbus, most of us recall the tales that were told to us in our youth. Rarely, if ever, do we take the time to reassess our knowledge of "the admiral of the ocean sea." It should be noted that some of our understandings are likely to be myths that grew up over the years out of strange stories never really understood by our young minds and now only dimly and inaccurately remembered.

It is commonly believed, for example, that Columbus and his crew were afraid of sailing off the surface of the earth, which they thought was flat. Pictures of Columbus convincing the navigators and churchmen of his time that this was not so still linger in our minds. Among intelligent men at the close of the fifteenth century, there was, of course, no question concerning the shape of the earth; its size, to be sure, was not known, but its general shape was a matter of common knowledge. There was no thought of sailing off the "edge" of the ocean that stretched west from Europe; there was, however, very real uncertainty about how far west men must go before finding land. With the limited amount of water and provisions then transportable, this was a critical factor. In this connection, Columbus himself miscalculated the distance and supposed that he would find "the Indies" somewhere beyond three thousand miles. It was this concern that very nearly persuaded Columbus to turn back on his first voyage when he was only a few days from the islands that signified the opening of the West.

It is also commonly believed that the learned people of his time scoffed at the thought of any success coming from his voyage. This is surely not true. A far more important factor was the success of Bartholomew Dias who had sailed around the tip of

Africa and so made at least an opening to "the Indies" possible, a route available for the first time for commerce and adventure.

Another notion that endures in the popular mind is the thought that Columbus and his companions were seeking wealth and plunder, that they were, like some later adventurers, out to make themselves rich. The truth is that many motives were involved, and not the least an evangelical one that sought to spread the gospel to new lands. Columbus himself was a religious man, and his trip was assisted in an important way by the Franciscan fathers who helped to arrange the presentation of his case to Queen Isabella of Spain. He always kept in mind a dedication to his patron, St. Christopher, and saw himself, among other things, as a "Christbearer" for his times.

Many who remember that Columbus sailed from Spain with a flagship and two caravels do not also recall that his journeys to the New World were four in number. While all of the trips had their moments of triumph and excitement, they also, alas, had their moments of disaster, and even something close to despair. The first discovery of San Salvador was followed by the exploration of parts of Cuba and a settlement on Hispaniola (Dominican Republic). Here a fort was established. On Christmas Day of 1492 the flagship was wrecked. As the new year dawned, Columbus left behind a small garrison and, with a number of Indians and some gold, set out in the *Nina* to return home with the news of his voyage. As the season suggests, they encountered storms and were driven toward the Azores, after which they sailed into Lisbon. It was a supreme irony that they should first greet the king of Portugal, from whom they had once sought support for their adventure only to be turned down. They proceeded on to Spain and the court at Barcelona, where a new expedition was immediately planned. Few people believed that the journey had truly found "the Indies," but everyone knew an historic discovery had been made.

In the fall of that same year, Columbus again set sail for the new land and by the end of November found the little port he had left behind. To his distress he found the total garrison gone, taken by death; he had to plan immediately a new site and a new settlement. At this time sickness overtook the hardy sailors as a result of infection, exhaustion, and the new and strange foods. Moreover, the skills of the navigator were not the skills of the administrator, and the colony was beset with trouble and disorder. Columbus, however, was able to explore further parts of Cuba and Jamaica before being recalled to Spain by a letter from the sovereign brought by Columbus's own brother, Bartholomew, who had arrived while Christopher was on exploration. He left a rather discontented colony and arrived in Spain in June of 1496.

The third voyage, which left Cape Verde in July of 1498, was the saddest of all. Columbus had asked for a chief justice from Spain to assist in ruling the colony. The justice arrived when the admiral and his brother were absent. On their arrival, however, they were put in chains and sent back to King Ferdinand. The humiliation was shortlived, and the king released the admiral.

It was not until 1502 that the last voyage of Columbus was made to the New World. This final journey was marked by illness, mutiny, mistreatment of the Indians, and finally the scuttling of the fleet in Jamaica because of shipworm damage to the hulls. Columbus and his men were marooned for more than a year before help came to them. Two weeks before Isabella's death in November 1504, Columbus arrived home. His own death came a scant two years later. He was fifty-five years old.

What does the story tell us that can bring meaning to the celebration of this day? Is it only a tale of adventure and daring, only a saga of courage and skill? There are deeper lessons here which the human heart in every age can ponder with profit.

There is, eminently, the lesson that not every great man receives, or should expect to receive, the rewards of his labors. Men today can recognize the talents and character of Columbus better than those who were closest to him. In the experience of life we judge one another harshly, so that very often men seem to be no greater than their greatest weakness. The admiral of the ocean sea was abused and put in chains not because he discovered America, but because his skills at colonization were vastly less than his skills of exploration. A hero is not a timeless figure; indeed, time very often is his greatest enemy. The ages will remember Colum-

bus, but those about him, most often for base reasons, were eager
to raise themselves up by bringing him down. Not even greatness
—exalted, visible, and unchallenged—walks the world without
withstanding the assaults of the mean, the petty, and the ignoble.
The strength of his nobility, however, brought to Columbus endur-
ance without rancor, and through it all, serenity.

Another lesson from the Columbus story is even more reassur-
ing. Columbus never found "the Indies"; indeed his calculations
were badly awry. But by patience, confidence, and courage he
made a greater discovery, greater even than he himself could
know. "There is a Providence that shapes our ends," the poet
tells us, and from this assurance men are transformed from human
frailty to men of destiny. The future is not ours to plan, only the
present. The eyes of men must be raised always to a horizon we
cannot see, to a work we do not know. This is the great lesson of
Columbus, a lesson rooted in faith, nurtured in hope, and confident in the goodness of God. In this spirit, America was discovered; in this spirit, under God, America must endure.

# IS THE UNITED NATIONS STILL OUR "LAST, BEST HOPE"?

*J. Robert Nelson*

*Professor of Systematic Theology, Boston University School of Theology; Member, United States National Commission for UNESCO; Chairman, Faith and Order Committee, World Council of Churches*

Why do the nations conspire,
    and the peoples plot in vain?
The kings of the earth set themselves,
    and the rulers take counsel together,
      against the Lord and his anointed, saying,
"Let us burst their bonds asunder, and cast their cords from us."

He who sits in the heavens laughs;
    the Lord has them in derision.
Then he will speak to them in his wrath,
    and terrify them in his fury, saying,
"I have set my king on Zion, my holy hill."

I will tell of the decree of the Lord:
He said to me, "You are my son,
    today I have begotten you.
Ask of me, and I will make the nations your heritage,
    and the ends of the earth your possession.
You shall break them with a rod of iron,
    and dash them in pieces like a potter's vessel."

Now therefore, O kings, be wise;
    be warned, O rulers of the earth.
Serve the Lord with fear,
    with trembling kiss his feet,
lest he be angry, and you perish in the way;
    for his wrath is quickly kindled.

Blessed are all who take refuge in him.

*Ps. 2*

What does the United Nations have to do with Georg Friedrich Händel's majestic oratorio, *The Messiah?* Externally, nothing. But internally there is a connection.

Each year the oratorio is sung by thousands of persons and heard by millions, never failing to please and inspire. The alto sings the words of Isaiah 53, applied since earliest times in Christian faith to Jesus: "He was despised, rejected, a man of sorrows and acquainted with grief." Then comes a musical meditation on the meaning of Jesus' death and Resurrection, culminating in the glorious "Hallelujah" chorus, which brings people spontaneously to their feet. But before this choral testimony to faith in Christ's victory over human corruption and nationalistic pride, the basso sings his strange aria from Psalm 2: "Why do the nations so furiously rage together, and the people imagine a vain thing?" Why indeed?

How do we understand this pathos of the nations which always speak of peace but make war? They talk of justice and humanity, but they exploit and oppress one another as they are able. Why? Is it not the international expression of the same moral problem with which each of us must struggle? Either we know what is good, as Paul confessed, but find some contrary, demonic power frustrating our intentions (Rom. 7:15), or we may in fact be those quarrelsome and avaricious persons who do not seriously want to do the good. So it is with nations as well.

When someone keeps professing commitment to goodwill and good works, our suspicions are aroused. How sincere is he? How genuinely committed? So we ask the nations of the world, too. Are security, peace, and well-being really at the top of their agenda? Or are such words just the facade of propaganda, concealing their real purposes? One test has been the willingness of nations to join in covenants for mutual aid and peace. Belligerent alliances, leagues, and treaties have been executed by the hundreds throughout history. These have had as their purpose either the common defense of signatory nations or their common conquest of others. Can the nations in similar way enter into, and abide by, covenants for the peace of all mankind?

Alfred Lord Tennyson, that sanguine poet of the Victorian British Empire, was inspired by the belief that the rise of democracy at home and the civilizing influence of the British around the world presaged an era of global peace. He dreamed and wrote of the coming Parliament of Man. Was it—even including Woman— an idle poetic dream?

Woodrow Wilson was the Presbyterian president whose Calvinism taught him not to underestimate human cussedness and sin. Still he believed that democracy would be kept in safety in a world held together by the biblical instrument of covenant: the League of Nations. But the Congress of his own government refused to sign the covenant. And even as the churches and secular groups of the twenties and thirties were uniting in efforts to justify Wilson's hopes, their disillusionment was ordained by the rise of totalitarian fascism and communism in Europe and militarism in Asia and America.

The nations still raged, and people imagined the vain idea that they were superior to all others.

Nevertheless, hope for securing peace by parliament does not die. Even in the midst of the war to prevent fascist Germany and imperial Japan from subduing most of the globe, in 1942 the plans for the United Nations were being laid. Inevitably the planners were the allied and neutral nations; but the long-range hope was that all would be included. They could not foresee just how numerous would be the "all" of the world by 1975. But in the mood of hopefulness tempered with realism, President Franklin D. Roosevelt prophesied that the United Nations could be "the last, best hope" for the peace of the world.

There are times in a person's life, as well as in a nation's, when dreamy idealism becomes an urgent necessity. Then much of our so-called realism—which is often just lack of confidence and hope —must be subordinated to the powerful, invigorating ideal. So it was for the nations in 1945. Representatives of fifty of them gathered in San Francisco to agree on the charter. It was signed on June 26. The great new instrument for world peace and justice was to become effective October 24.

In this uncertain life something unexpected may always be expected. The same President Harry S Truman who opened the San

Francisco conference decided to put into destructive use the most awesome creation of modern science, the atomic bomb. The United Nations charter was signed in the prenuclear age. It became effective while Hiroshima and Nagasaki were still smoldering piles of radioactive ruin. Moreover, the charter was signed while the United States and the Soviet Union were teamed in the last months of the hot war. By the time the United Nations began, the relations of the two great allies were turning to cold war. In retrospect on 1945, can we not say it was in the providence of God that the nations had come together just in the nick of time? But would their frail structure survive the stress of the postwar years?

For three decades it has not only survived, but to a higher degree than many think has been serving its purposes. It has provided the means for preventing some disputes between raging nations from becoming wars. In Korea, 1950, the youthful United Nations itself had to engage in war against aggression from the north. For years it has kept the lid on the Middle Eastern pot, often threatening to boil over. The controls on armaments, especially nuclear weapons, may not seem to be very tight today. But what would it be like without such controls as have been agreed upon through arbitration? More successful than political settlements have been the humanitarian actions. Refugees by the millions in this "century of the homeless man" have been aided and resettled. International funds for economic development of Third World nations are disbursed through the World Bank and several agencies. The Food and Agriculture Organization provides a way for common action against hunger. World consciousness about human rights, women's rights, ecological threats, and population crisis has been raised by United Nations programs. And through UNESCO the cause of peace is served by the means of educational, cultural, and scientific ventures. Not to have these international channels would now seem unthinkable.

These achievements stand, despite failures. But now the United Nations is in trouble, and it will no doubt live with the same troubles for some years to come.

Critics point out the devastating fact that many wars have been fought since 1945, in spite of the peaceful purpose and availability of the United Nations. The names still have an ominous ring: Korea, Indonesia, Israel, Congo (Katanga), Nigeria (Biafra), the Sudan, Algeria, Cyprus, Pakistan, Bangladesh, Laos, Cambodia, Vietnam. And the United Nations has been helpless in face of the military suppressions in Hungary, Czechoslovakia, Angola, and Southwest Africa (Namibia). In some of these conflicts the United States has had a huge commercial stake; in some, a political stake. And certain opponents of the United Nations claim that the world organization is a hindrance and threat to American interests. The eminent historian, Henry Steele Commager, refutes them by insisting we cannot solve world problems on our own, but must work in and through the United Nations. Until now, on major matters the United States has ignored it, he claims.*

More difficult for American interests than the go-it-alone mentality is the glaring reality of the shift of voting power. The number of member states has nearly tripled since the fifty gathered at the Golden Gate. Where did they all come from? Forty-seven are former colonies of Great Britain. Others have arisen by liberation and new alignments in Africa, the Middle East, the Caribbean and Pacific Isles. As each new nation, however small, comes into being, it qualifies for membership; and each has one vote. The vote of Malawi or Grenada is equal to that of India or the United States. And it is plain as sunrise that the more new nations take seats in the General Assembly, the greater is the majority opposed to the North Atlantic nations. The latter could not block the seating of the People's Republic of China, in place of the Nationalist government of Taiwan (Republic of China), nor attacks on South Africa, nor the tacit acceptance of the nonnation Palestine Liberation Organization. For modern powers like Britain, France, and the United States, this is not merely humiliating. It seems in the eyes of many that the actions of many small nations are subverting the high purpose of the United Nations, stifling reasoned debate, turning the General Assembly into a spawning ground of acrimonious resolutions, and paralyzing the constructive work of the executive staff. On the other hand, this surely demonstrates the impact of a sudden, massive revolution in human history. Coloni-

* *Boston Globe*, 4 May 1975, p. B1.

alism of political genus is dead.  Only a few instances like Hong
Kong remain.  White people, still the richest and most powerful,
though a minority, are irrevocably on the defensive.  And the
several varieties of socialism—from Maoism to Russian Marxism-
Leninism to the democratic systems of Sweden and the Nether-
lands—are ascendant.

It is pointless to preach about the United Nations and extol its
pacific mystique without taking these controversial data into account.  But some might reasonably demand, Why *preach* on this
subject?  Why should the *churches* observe October 24?  Christian sermons are supposed to present the gospel of Jesus Christ.
The gospel is a religious message.  Isn't the United Nations simply
a political concern?

By no means!

There is a difference between an interpretive or promotional
lecture about the United Nations and a sermon on it.  The agnos-
tic or atheist may be just as zealous a supporter of the United
Nations as any Christian; both are committed to the cause of peace
and human justice.

The difference lies in their understandings of two things: the
motive *power* and the ultimate *purpose* of this singular instrument
in human history.  And these two have four implications for Christian faith:

1. The gospel is intensely personal when it is believed and
appropriated as God's working in Jesus Christ for the reconciliation and full life of men and women.  Moreover, by the gospel, the
community of the church is built up; so the church throughout
the world, when true to its nature, is "the sign and instrument of the
coming unity of mankind."*  Still further, the Christian interpreta-
tion of human life includes the whole range of humanity in all
time.  It sees history on the grand scale as the theater where God's
creatures are working out their eternal destiny.  In other and sim-
pler words, Christians can discern in the United Nations more than
an urgent political measure devised by politicians and diplomats.
They see an unprecedented and perhaps unrepeatable opportunity

* A concept adopted by both the Second Vatican Council and the Assembly of
the World Council of Churches.

for all nations and people to move towards that era of mutuality and peace which is symbolized by Jesus' preaching of the kingdom of God.

2. Christian faith also prevents us from falling prey to naive optimism. From the Old Testament come the clearest warnings against national pride, arrogance, and aggressiveness. As Psalm 2 declares, when the nations rage violently against his will, God laughs. He holds them in derision. He knows that, despite the nations' destructive powers, they cannot prevail against his ultimate purpose; nor can their protestations of goodwill, unbacked by policies and deeds, deceive God or ourselves.

3. Yet, God continually guides and aids the nations towards peace. He not only laughs, but he judges; not only judges, but shows compassion. God uses myriad ways of continually reminding human beings that the joys of freedom, justice, dignity, and love are for *all* people; not for one people, one race, one nation, one region, or any cluster of them, but for all. Even as God created "from one every nation of men to live on all the face of the earth" (Acts 17:26), so in Jesus Christ he gave himself in love for the benefit of everyone who lives.

4. And therein, lastly, lies our hope. Our hope for a peaceful world does not reside in the United Nations as such, but in God's will. Yet the United Nations is surely a major, indispensable tool which is used for that realization. As the God of history, rather than a remote deity or diffused spirit, he penetrates our finite, earthly sphere and turns even our futile mistakes and the raging of nations to his purpose. It is faithless and contrary to biblical teaching, therefore, to hold that the United Nations has no place in God's will. Christians should give thanks for it, help it in its weakness, and rejoice in its strength.

Every great movement or institution needs a personification, an incarnation. The foremost personage of the first thirty years of the United Nations has been Dag Hammarskjöld. This modest, reflective Swede had been introduced by his father to the churches' ecumenical movement in 1925. He knew with an unusual clarity and profundity what Jesus Christ meant for each person and for human history at large. After his untimely death in 1961 in

Katanga, while in line of duty as a peacemaker, his diary of intimate thoughts was discovered and published as *Markings*. One simple entry of 1945 comprehends the whole meaning of the organization and cause he served so well: "No peace which is not peace for all, no rest until all has been fulfilled."

# POLITICS AND FREEDOM

*Cynthia C. Wedel*

*Member of the Presidium, World Council of Churches;*
*National Chairperson of Volunteers, American Red Cross*

Then he said to them, "Render therefore to Caesar the things that are Caesar's, and to God the things that are God's."

Matt. 22:21

One of the significant features of the Judeo-Christian religious tradition is that it takes "the world" seriously. Many other religious faiths, or systems by which people have lived, have been basically "world-denying," looking upon worldly matters as intrinsically evil—sometimes even denying their reality altogether, in an overemphasis on the "spiritual."

The Christian church, following the Jewish roots from which it grew, has always rejected such dualism. Beginning with the story of the Creation in Genesis, it is made clear that God created the universe and everything in it. The creation of matter—of earth and waters, plants and animals—is not only spelled out in detail, but each act of creation is concluded with the lovely refrain "and God saw that it was good." Obviously, the almighty Creator of heaven and earth enjoyed his handiwork and was pleased with it. If this is so, it is certainly wrong for finite human beings to imply that any part of God's creation is unworthy or outside his loving concern.

This would also seem to indicate that the "dominion" over the things of the earth, which the same ancient story tells us God gave to his human children, is important to the Creator. How we organize and structure our societies to exercise this dominion in a responsible way must, therefore, be of concern to God. Even so obviously secular and political an issue as a system of government and a political election are matters for which the people of God must feel a religious responsibility.

94

In a period of rapid change and turmoil such as the present, the church needs to be reminding its members—and the citizenry at large—that government is under the rule of God and that the exercise of the franchise is an essential part of government. It is a part of fulfilling our Lord's command to "render unto Caesar the things that are Caesar's."

One problem resulting from the church becoming involved in the political process is the danger, pointed out dramatically by many competent theologians in recent years, of the development of an American civil religion. At its most serious stage, this can take the form of substituting America, or the American way of life, for God—an often unconscious, but real form of idolatry. The growth and prosperity of the United States is seen as an indication of a special providence. American values and customs are equated with God's values and the way God likes things done. A kind of uncritical loyalty and devotion is demanded, analogous to the uncomplaining submission to the will of God which can be seen in a devoutly religious person.

Recognizing this very real hazard, it still seems worthwhile to think about what God may have had in mind for his human children in terms of a structure of society. Here, again, we can go back to the story of Creation. In Genesis 1:27 we are told that "God created man in his own image." This is the unique thing about human beings in contrast to all the rest of creation. We alone, as far as we know, are the part of creation which is "like" God. Human beings seem, in the biblical narrative, to be those for whose sake all the rest of creation was established and those to whom the rule was given.

What does "the image of God" mean? We are too sophisticated to think that it means we look like God. Some have suggested that we alone in creation have the power to reason, to invent, to remember, and to foresee the future. But more significant than any of these qualities, God actually made us free. He shared with us the freedom which he has. We are free to make choices, to do good or evil, to obey or disobey our Creator. We are free even to deny his existence.

God, being God, must have known that we would use our freedom, including disobeying him, in much the same way that Adam and Eve used their freedom in the garden. The story of Adam and Eve can be seen as a parable or allegory of the temptation which all human beings face of wanting to "be like God" and to exercise our freedom by doing *our* will and forcing it on others.

The whole course of human history can be seen as a narrative of people seeking freedom and power for themselves and denying it to others. The ancient world quickly devised hierarchical systems for government, religion, education, and the family, in which one person or a very small elite group with power, wealth, or knowledge became the rulers, at the top of the pyramid, and everyone else was assigned a place below them and was expected to do what he or she was told. As human society developed, new institutions such as business and industry followed the same pattern. The great majority of humankind had no real freedom.

When these hierarchical structures were benevolent, the results were not too disastrous. The masses of humanity, largely uneducated, very poor, and burdened with hard physical labor just to scratch out a meager existence, were generally thankful for the protection and stability which such a society provided. Freedom would have been a luxury for which they had neither the knowledge, time, nor energy. When hierarchies were tyrannical and cruel, which they often were, the lot of the masses could be wretched, but they had neither the ability nor the opportunity to rebel.

It seems very possible that this ordering of society was contrary to God's will, even though it was often justified with religious sanctions such as the divine right of kings. Jesus said and did many things which indicated that the law of God and the will of God were far more important than the laws and governments devised by human power. It was precisely this challenging of the power structure of his day which finally brought him to the cross. The Resurrection has always been seen by Christians not only as an indication of eternal life, but as a sign of God's victory over all the force and power of human society.

It is possible to make a very good case for the hypothesis that, in creating us free, God hoped for a society in which people would, indeed, all be free—free to make their own decisions, free to choose the form of government they wanted, and free to make the laws which would permit the society to function. The combination of human sin and self-centeredness and the ignorance and poverty of the majority of human beings in earlier ages seemed to make God's plan an impossibility. It is often hard for us to understand why our Creator is so patient, why he allows us to act as we do. Obviously, God has chosen to limit himself and not intervene directly in human history. Yet, the Bible is full of the words of prophets and sages, and of Jesus and his followers, who have tried to communicate God's will. But human beings were not ready to hear.

It is only within the past few centuries, in the slow working out of God's plan for his children, that the conditions of human life have begun to change and that freedom for the many is becoming more possible. Education, often brought by the church, has slowly spread to more and more people. God began to allow men to discover some of the secrets of the universe, and modern science began. From science has come the technology which, with all its faults, has opened new vistas of life to races and nations. Millions of people in every part of the world are for the first time breaking out of old isolation, learning about other people, acquiring knowledge, information, and skills which are freeing them from the bondage of ignorance and toil. It is as though God has decided that the time has come to extend freedom to all his children.

If this is indeed God's will, it places upon each of us as Christians a responsibility to do anything we can to help further it. We need to become aware of those people in our world for whom freedom is still impossible because of poverty or ignorance or injustice and to find ways in which we can help them overcome these barriers.

We can also recall with profound gratitude the founders of our own nation who, two centuries ago, had the faith and the courage to design a form of government which was based on the will of the governed. Although in the beginning the right to vote was limited to certain groups, the democratic processes of our system made it possible to amend the rules until today we have almost universal adult suffrage. God's great gift of freedom—to choose, to help shape one's own destiny—is more available to us as Americans than it has ever been to any people at any place or time in history.

How tragic it is, then, to read the statistics of the great numbers of us who do not bother to vote! Surely this indicates more than just political apathy. It reveals ignorance of how precious freedom is and of the fact that we must exercise our freedom if we are to keep it. But, even more serious, is the fact that failure to participate in our democratic system suggests a lack of gratitude to God for the fundamental gift of freedom with which he has endowed us.

As we approach this election day, let us each resolve to take with the utmost seriousness our responsibility as Christians to accept gratefully God's gift of freedom and use it to help shape and guide our own country; and let us urge those to whom we give the power of government to use it to advance the freedom of all people everywhere. God grant that "the glorious liberty of the children of God" may become a reality in our time.

# THE PEACE OF CHRIST

*Ronald J. Sider*

*Associate Professor of History and Religion, Messiah College, Philadelphia; Chairperson, Evangelicals for Social Action*

But now in Christ Jesus you who once were far off have been brought near in the blood of Christ. For he is our peace, who has made us both one, and has broken down the dividing wall of hostility, by abolishing in his flesh the law of commandments and ordinances, that he might create in himself one new man in place of the two, so making peace, and might reconcile us both to God in one body through the cross, thereby bringing the hostility to an end.

Eph. 2:13–16

Veterans Day prompts painful memories of courageous men and women who died, they hoped, for the sake of peace. Many times in this century American leaders have summoned our best youth into battle to produce a lasting peace. But still—in spite of some decades relatively free of major conflict—lasting peace evades us.

What is peace? Is there perhaps a difference between the peace of Christ and the peace proclaimed by our culture and national leaders? What is the peace of Christ?

Paul described the peace of Christ in our text. There are two aspects of the peace of Christ here. The one part is the vertical peace with God through faith in Jesus who died for us. The other aspect of the peace of Christ is a new radical kind of horizontal peace which crashes through all the dividing walls—age, sex, race, nation, color—which people erect to keep other persons at a distance.

What is the essence of the vertical peace with God? We have been brought near and reconciled to God through the blood of Christ on the cross. Paul sums it up beautifully in Romans 5:1: "Therefore since we are justified by faith, we have peace with God through our Lord Jesus Christ."

99

Proud sinful persons would always prefer to earn their own justification before God by their own efforts and good life. Sometimes we try to earn our own righteousness by being good citizens and living moral lives; sometimes we try to do it by our piety and offerings to the church. But God says no! All human efforts to earn God's favor are mere filthy rags.

Thank God there is another way to peace with God. We can have peace with God because we are justified by faith alone (Rom. 4:5). If we simply confess our sin and throw ourselves on God's mercy in Christ, we have peace with God.

If this vertical peace with God were all there were to the peace of Christ, that in itself would be wonderful. But there is more. The peace of Christ also includes a horizontal peace with other believers. The Jews and Gentiles were two hostile, cultural, national groups. But in Christ, these two groups of people who had hated and despised each other and even fought wars against each other are now reconciled. Christ has created one new man, one new body of believers, in place of the two hostile groups.

The same thing is true in the case of men and women, slaves and masters, Greeks and barbarians. Since all are accepted before God on precisely the same basis, they are equal in Christ. That is why Paul repeatedly tells us that in Christ all racial barriers, all sexual barriers, all age barriers, all cultural barriers are abolished. As a barrier-breaker the peace of Christ is a wellspring of nonconformity in a much-divided world.

God calls his church today to be a nonconformist community. We should not be conformed to this world's views of black persons, Indians, women, Russians, draft evaders, poor people, the elderly. Instead, our churches should be visible demonstrations of the fact that God's love flows equally to people of all classes, races, and ages. Because we have peace with God through the cross, our congregations should be visible communities where peace between hostile groups is already a reality.

On Veterans Day particularly, we cannot avoid a very hard question: How does all of this relate to the problem of war and violence? If Christ brings vertical peace with God and horizontal peace with the brothers and sisters in the church, does he also offer Christians a new way to relate to war and violence?

Jesus' approach to violent persons was to suffer rather than inflict suffering, to endure the cross rather than use the dagger. "You have heard that it was said 'an eye for an eye and a tooth for a tooth.' But I say to you, do not resist one who is evil. But if anyone strikes you on the right cheek, turn to him the other also.... I say to you love your enemies and pray for those who persecute you" (Matt. 5:38–44). Paul summed it all up beautifully in Romans 12:19–21: "Beloved, never avenge yourselves, but leave it to the wrath of God.... If your enemy is hungry, feed him; if he is thirsty, give him drink.... Do not be overcome by evil, but overcome evil with good." And in 1 Peter, the apostle calls on Christians to endure unfair attacks patiently: "If when you do right and suffer for it you take it patiently, you have God's approval. For to this you have been called, because Christ also suffered for you, leaving you an example, that you should follow in his steps" (1 Pet. 2:20–21). The Bible specifically commands Christians to suffer rather than inflict suffering and violence.

Many people today accept Jesus' way of nonviolence as a beautiful ideal. But they feel that in practice it is unrealistic and impractical. In a world infested with Hitlers, Stalins, and colonists with guns, persons and nations who follow the way of the cross get wiped out. So one must sadly fight wars to preserve justice and restore peace.

The most forceful way I know to respond to this very convincing argument is to return to the New Testament conception of the implication of Jesus' Resurrection. When Jesus came preaching the good news of the kingdom of heaven, he naturally aroused the messianic hope that the new age of peace and justice was at hand. According to messianic expectation, the dead would be resurrected and the Spirit would be poured out when the new age arrived.

Now Jesus went about Palestine announcing the fantastic news that the kingdom of heaven was at hand. He insisted that the kingdom was already beginning in his ministry wherever people became his followers, forsook the values of Satan's kingdom, and started living the values of a very different kingdom. The early church also believed and taught that the new age had begun—precisely because of Jesus' Resurrection. They knew, of course, that the kingdom would come in its fullness only at Christ's return.

But the Resurrection was a visible sign that it made sense to begin living according to the standards of the new age which had already invaded the old age.

The majority of people, of course, still live by the standards of the old era. But the life-style of Christians ought to be a living proof of their belief that the new age has started. Christians do not claim that we should wait to live by the kingdom's standards on lying, theft, or adultery until non-Christians stop lying, stealing, and fornicating. Nor should the church delay implementing Jesus' nonviolent method of overcoming evil with good until the Caesars and Hitlers disappear.

The Resurrection stands as God's tangible sign that implementing Jesus' nonviolent ethics now is not a foolish imitation of a visionary fanatic, but rather a sane submission to the one who is Lord of heaven and earth. That the Resurrection was the decisive clue to Jesus' identity is clear in every strand of early Christian literature. Before the Resurrection, the disciples called him master and rabbi; afterward they said, "My Lord and my God." Repeatedly in Acts, the text makes it clear that it was the Resurrection that led the disciples to confess Jesus of Nazareth as Messiah and Lord (Acts 2:32–36; 5:30–31).

If Jesus of Nazareth is the Messiah, then surely one simply obeys. If the one who called his followers to love their enemies is the Lord of the universe, then surely any attempt to circumvent or ignore his teaching is unthinkable.

One powerful objection to this understanding of the peace of Christ must be considered. Does biblical nonviolence represent mere passivity and neutrality in the face of evil? Sadly we must confess that "pacifist" Christians sometimes have also been passive. But there is no justification for passivity and neutrality in the Bible. Jesus as always is our model. He denounced evil Pharisees with a passion. And when he went to cleanse the temple, he grabbed a whip, drove the animals out of the temple, and threw the money changers' tables upside down.

How often do the people in our church engage in that kind of demonstration for the sake of justice and peace? Notice that Jesus did not kill the money changers; he probably did not even whip them. But he was not passive and neutral. I think that means, to cite a contemporary example, that the Christian may use nonviolent techniques to resist apartheid in South Africa. The nonviolent Christian in South Africa will realize just as clearly as the armed guerrilla that there is no neutral position. Taking no stand has the same effect as supporting the present evil. But the Christian will not dehumanize or kill the oppressor. Instead he will use Jesus' method, which enables him to love the oppressor and treat him as a person precisely at the same time that he opposes his evil, unjust actions. Biblical nonviolence is not at all the same as neutral passivity. The peace that Christ brings, then, involves not only a vertical peace with God and a horizontal peace with the brothers and sisters in the church; it also includes a new nonviolent alternative to war and violence.

One of the tragedies of our age is that the two aspects of peace, the vertical relationship with God and the horizontal peace with our neighbors, have been rent asunder. Some humanists and liberal Christians thought they could have Jesus as a happy modern peacemaker between races and nations, even though they ignored his death on the cross and the new birth through the Holy Spirit. But it won't work. We cannot follow the way of the cross in our own efforts. We must have the revolutionary transforming power of the Holy Spirit flowing through us if we want to live the Jesus way. And a sure enduring peace between hostile groups is possible only when it is built on the foundation of forgiveness and acceptance with God through the cross.

But humanists and liberal Christians are not the only ones who have tried to pick and choose those things in Christ's peace that they find appealing. Far too many theologically "orthodox" Christians suppose that they can seek forgiveness of sins and obtain peace with God, and then ignore Jesus' teaching that his disciples will love their enemies and leave vengeance to God. It is simply impossible to have peace with God and then turn around and say, "thank you, but I'd rather not obey quite all your commands." Acceptance with God is totally free, but it is never separated from unconditional submission to Jesus as Lord. And Jesus will not be Lord of half of our lives. If we want to have peace with God through Jesus' cross, then we must joyfully accept him as Lord of every area of our lives—of our sexual practices, of our homes, of our spending, of our economics, of our politics. He must be Lord even of our sinful desire to fight rather than suffer, to kill rather than be killed.

Let us all renew our pledge to God that we want Jesus to be absolute Lord of our lives. And as we do that, Christ brings us his peace. Constantly he fills us with the joyful certainty that we have eternal peace with the just Lord of the universe through the cross. And then precisely as we experience that abiding peace, we discover that he frees us to work for peace on earth.

# WHAT IS YOUR GRATITUDE LEVEL?

*R. H. Edwin Espy*

*Chairman, Project Forward '76;*
*Former General Secretary, National Council of Churches*

Make a joyful noise to the Lord, all the lands!
Serve the Lord with gladness!
 Come into his presence with singing!

Know that the Lord is God!
 It is he that made us, and we are his;
 we are his people, and the sheep of his pasture.

Enter his gates with thanksgiving,
 and his courts with praise!
 Give thanks to him, bless his name!

For the Lord is good;
 his steadfast love endures for ever,
 and his faithfulness to all generations.

Ps. 100

Of all our national holidays, Thanksgiving is the one that is committed uniquely to gratitude. It began in 1621 when the Plymouth colony instituted a special day of prayer and thanksgiving following a successful harvest.

In due course, Thanksgiving became an annual observance which spread to other colonies and states. In 1864 Abraham Lincoln made it a national holiday and issued the first proclamation calling upon the people to give thanks to God for the nation's blessings.

Thus Thanksgiving Day in a unique way is more than a day of commemoration of something that happened in the distant past. It is an occasion for doing again what our forefathers did more than 350 years ago. We remember the prayers of the Pilgrims, but we engage in prayer ourselves. We express again our grati-

105

tude for the mercies of a Divine Providence embracing all that has happened to us, good and bad, right down to the present day.

This makes Thanksgiving difficult. Many perceptive and dedicated people quite appropriately hesitate. How can we be so thankful, they ask, when there has been such pain and suffering? Or even harder, how can we pretend to be grateful when our history has been so spotty, such a mixture of good and evil? For the truth must be faced: Despite our glorious heritage, we have committed sins as a nation, both in our dealings with many of our own people and in some of our relations with other nations.

Today we have reason to be especially penitent. We are more mindful of our shortcomings in this modern era of investigation and communication. Not only have the victims of our misdeeds, at home and abroad, become articulate in their protests, but the probing eyes of the public information media and official government agencies have brought our misdeeds to view. The whole world is aware that we are guilty of corruption and abuse of power.

Is it not hypocritical, therefore, to pretend to be grateful for such a record? How can we give thanks to God for patent and blatant wrongdoing? Is this not the God of Israel, who desired that "justice roll down like waters, and righteousness like a mighty stream?" Can we still be truly thankful?

The answer is a resounding yes! The reasons are many, but we shall focus on three.

First, there is the biblical experience. It finds expression supremely in the Psalms where the theme of gratitude and rejoicing is paramount. Psalm 100 is a single example: "Enter his gates with thanksgiving, and his courts with praise! Give thanks to him, bless his name."

Men were to thank their God for protection and guidance of his people not because of their successes, but in spite of their sufferings and failures. Nor was their gratitude based on a record of unfailing obedience to the divine will. Did ever a people hear itself exposed and excoriated for its sins so profusely across the centuries as did the people of Israel by the tongues of its prophets? Their voice was the voice of God, who knew their waywardness far better than they knew it themselves, yet never broke off his covenant relationship. They continued to be his people, and he continued to expect their thanksgiving and praise.

The life of Christ was a symphony of gratitude. Never do we find him, even in greatest extremity, removed from his identity with God. He expressed it in love and obedience and praise. In what was perhaps his most sacred utterance, the high priestly prayer on the eve of his Crucifixion, we find him spilling out his gratitude—gratitude for God's gift in the disciples and supplication to God that he will continue them in his favor and protection (John 17).

In a day when we are groping for values, when the traditional virtues seem to be wearing thin, is there any sentiment more elemental, more ennobling of our relationships—across all the lines of faith and race and culture and class and political belief—than gratitude?

This, however, does not take us as far as we must go. The kind of gratitude required of us for Thanksgiving Day is made of even sterner stuff. Our gratitude must be tempered with confession and selectivity.

We make no claim to perfection in our national history. As loyal Americans it is part of our duty to be honest critics. We must guard against the temptation to use Thanksgiving Day as an occasion of undifferentiated praise. Numerous religious and other bodies have warned against the danger, indeed the dishonesty, of hiding our national faults and injustices. They insist, in the words of the National Council of Churches, that "the shortcomings of the nation be recognized and rectified."

There is, of course, nothing revolutionary in this reminder. It is a simple affirmation of the necessity of discrimination in our loyalties. To celebrate Thanksgiving does not call for undifferentiated approval of everything in our history or everything in our present life as a people. On the contrary, it provides an occasion to reflect, to assess, to select, and to reject—all in the spirit of gratitude.

Each American should make his own assessment of his country's history, informed and enlightened by the facts. This is in the nature of a democratic society. The responsibility in the final analysis falls upon the individual. This is an ancient insight which was embodied in the life of our nation and calls for constant reaffirmation.

Ours is a land of freedom. But we often forget this fact. We confront so many perplexities that freedom comes to seem unreal, an abstraction drowned out by reality. Thanksgiving Day observance should prompt us to dig more deeply at the roots of our liberty.

The most basic of our freedoms is religious freedom, on which all our other freedoms rest. Freedom is a question of human values, which are rooted in God. It is good that discerning contemporaries in the leadership of thought and action in our society acknowledge and reiterate this incontestable fact.

In the political realm, we have the simple testimony of Nelson A. Rockefeller before the Senate committee that was examining his qualifications for the vice-presidency. In helping his inquisitors to understand that he was something more than a man of wealth and politics, that he had other roots and values, he focused on a singular theme. He was the child, he said, of forebears who had come to this country first and foremost for religious freedom. Religious freedom!

The blessings of America are many. The abuses and misuses of our blessings are also abundant. It is not the part of gratitude either to idealize our life or to debunk it, but to come to it in honest gratitude, the kind of gratitude that discriminates, that "tests the spirits to see whether they be of God." This is not a vapid nationalism. "Nationalism," Albert Einstein reminds us, "is an infantile disease; it is the measles of mankind." Discriminating gratitude, the true patriotism, is a higher sentiment.

It all comes down, in short, to the perception and fidelity of the individual. Each of us should put to himself or herself some very personal questions:

—What is my gratitude level?

—Am I truly grateful to the God whose will it was that this nation should be born and who has been with us on the way?

—Do I practice the kind of contagious personal gratitude that makes me a better human being, a better neighbor, and a better citizen of my country?

—Am I able to discriminate in giving thanks for America, affirming what is good, deploring what is bad, making confession of our sins, and striving always for "liberty and justice for all"?

If the answers to these questions are affirmative, Thanksgiving Day can be a real celebration.

# THE ROLE OF RELIGION IN AMERICA

*Joseph L. Bernardin*

*Archbishop of Cincinnati;*
*President, National Conference of Catholic Bishops*

Thanksgiving is one of our most cherished national festivals. On this day our religious and civic heritages come together in a special way, inspiring us to turn our thoughts and prayers in gratitude to the beneficent Creator who has so blessed this land and its people. It is a time, too, for us to ponder seriously our national values and commitments and to do so in the light of our religious tradition. The religious tradition is not the only voice to be heard in the continuing public dialogue about our purposes as a nation, but it is a voice which must be heard, because it has things to tell us which are of profound importance for our national life.

Even as I say this, I am aware that organized religion does not play precisely the same role in national life that it has played at times in the past. There are those who believe that, because the role of organized religion has changed, religion itself has therefore diminished in importance as a social institution. I do not believe that this is precisely the case. It may very well be true that the churches today do not have the same direct, immediate impact on society that they have had at other times in our history. Yet they do have a real impact, exerted primarily through their formative influence on the values and attitudes of those who are their members. Because this is difficult to quantify, it is easy to overlook. Our fondness for what is measurable—for what can be reduced to statistics or charted on graphs—should not blind us to the powerful part that ideas and symbols, including the ideas and symbols of religion, play in the lives of individuals and nations. On this profound level, not easily accessible to polls and instruments of empirical investigation, religion has always had, and continues to have, its most significant impact on national life.

Along with this, however, it is necessary to acknowledge a certain diminution in the role of organized religion in our country in recent decades and a corresponding increase in the role played by another phenomenon to which the name "civil religion" has been given. One need not accept in all particulars the elaborate parallels worked out by some between traditional religion and civil religion in order to recognize the basic truth of what they are saying. Public life must necessarily be organized around a system of value-laden symbols, and, in a pluralistic and increasingly secularized country such as our own, it is natural that a significant part of this role should be played by figures, institutions, and events of a broadly "political" character. To the degree that civil religion helps to give continuity, coherence, and purposefulness to our public life, it serves an essential purpose. In many ways the observance of Thanksgiving itself is an example of what is best in the tradition of American civil religion.

Nevertheless it is possible for abuses to be perpetrated under the cloak of civil religion. This happens when its symbols are manipulated—by the misguided or the unscrupulous—in order to conceal unworthy motives and vicious policies. It is at this point that we become painfully conscious of the fact that civil religion, while necessary, is also radically inadequate. Without awareness that our nation stands under higher judgment, the judgment embodied in the ideas and symbols of theistic religion, the tradition of civil religion is positively dangerous.

I wish to mention in particular three areas in which the symbols of our civil religion are perhaps particularly susceptible to manipulation and abuse, calling for judgment and correction by the higher values of theistic religion.

One is the tendency to think of America and Americans as enjoying a kind of privileged moral superiority by comparison with other nations and peoples. At various times in American history, this notion—that we are a new chosen people—has led us to indulge ourselves in such abuses as racism and nativism. Bigotry is part of the dark side of the American character—although generosity is equally a part of that character.

A second area which should be of deep concern to all of us is

our national fondness for violence. The Minuteman, the fron-
tierman, the cowboy, the GI are mythic figures of our civil religion
—rightfully so. Yet the values and virtues they symbolize—self-
reliance, courage, devotion to duty—are sometimes given less
prominence than the brutal notion that they were men who, when
the chips were down, knew how to settle problems with a gun.
This idea is deep-rooted and persistent in American life. Popular
culture consistently panders to our addiction to violence. The
statistics on gun ownership, legal and illegal, by private citizens in
the United States are truly staggering—as, for that matter, are the
statistics on violent crime committed with these same weapons.
After years of debate, we seem no more able to divest ourselves of
handguns than to cure the common cold. Is it because the legal
and constitutional issues are really so complex? Or is it also
because of what the gun and its relationship to violence symbolize
for us on some darker level of the national psyche?

Similarly, at various times in our history, our international relationships have seemed to be based on the assumption that violence
is a cure-all. I do not question the proposition that, in this very
imperfect world, it may sometimes be necessary for a nation, as
for an individual, to resort to force in order to vindicate certain
rights. Yet if we have learned nothing else from the experience of
Vietnam, we should have learned that violence is not the answer to
every problem and that winning minds and hearts is not ultimately
accomplished by guns, bombs, and napalm. We must be prepared
as a nation to respond intelligently to challenges on the level of
ideas and ideologies, values and commitments. We cannot rely
exclusively on military power, however necessary it may be, to
promote our valid national interests and serve our national purposes.

A third area of concern involves the ambivalence of our attitudes toward relationships with other nations. Much of our history has been marked by the predominance of one or the other of
two extremes: on the one hand, a sometimes messianic commitment to "manifest destiny" or some equivalent thereof; on the
other hand, isolationism, aloofness, and withdrawal from international involvements—almost as if these would be a source of

moral contamination to us. Yet side by side with these attitudes, America's international record also reflects great generosity and a proper sense of commitment to our real duties in the world. Let us hope that, as the post-Vietnam reassessment of our international role proceeds, this aspect of our tradition will be emphasized. Our foreign policies in the years ahead should properly be defined in terms of interdependence and our obligation, in view of our national power and wealth, to play a truly exemplary role on the world scene.

We cannot, however, simply take it for granted that what is best in our tradition will prevail during this present period of restudy and reassessment. On the contrary, the confusion and uncertainty manifest in many areas of national life today create the conditions in which manipulation of the symbols of civil religion is all too easy and all too possible. At such a moment we should be particularly wary of the danger of demagoguery—whether of the left or the right—which would cloak itself in the symbols of civil religion in order to appeal to our selfishness and baser instincts.

Rational, principled discourse, not demagoguery, is an urgent national need today. In particular, we must be respectful of what all responsible groups have to contribute to the ongoing national dialogue. It would be tragic if the building of a new national consensus in fact degenerated into a version of the tyranny of the majority, in which hard sayings—including those spoken by persons addressing national issues from the perspective of the religious tradition—were shouted down and denied a hearing. We have heard much, even from our Supreme Court, about the evils of religious "divisiveness." But it would be a far greater evil if any responsible group, including persons of religious commitment, were denied an effective opportunity to address public issues because of the fancied danger of divisiveness.

As I have suggested, civil religion by itself is not capable of supplying the principles and values necessary for determining the course of public policy in our nation. The symbols of civil religion are an important part of our tradition, but they must be animated by the principles of other value systems. It is at this point that our religious tradition properly comes into play.

I do not mean to suggest that in the last analysis religion should dictate public policy. This would be both impossible and unacceptable. But religion does provide a normative system of values against which our behavior as individuals and our corporate behavior as a society should be measured. To use an old-fashioned word, this is a question of conscience—and conscience, formed by religious values and commitments, is an essential part of our lives both as individuals and as a nation.

Describing and putting into practice the proper relationship of the religious tradition to national life is not a simple matter in times like ours—times marked by the secularization of society, by religious and ideological pluralism, and by controversy and confusion over church-state questions. It is essential, however, that there be a rich, deep relationship marked by vitality and healthy interaction. Important as civil religion may be, it does not and cannot substitute in national life for the contributions of authentic religious values and commitments. In this time of national reassessment in particular, the nation would risk being rudderless—or, even worse, being propelled into false choices and dangerous courses—if it were to rely solely on the symbols of civil religion, symbols too easily manipulated for unworthy purposes. Let it be our Thanksgiving prayer that, in the present and the future, as in the past, our nation will draw inspiration and purpose from the abiding insights of our religious traditions.

# THE BIBLICAL HERITAGE AND HUMAN RIGHTS

*Marc H. Tanenbaum*

*Director, Interreligious Affairs, American Jewish Committee;
Co-Chairman, Interreligious Coalition on World Hunger*

There is no word for religion in the Hebrew Bible. And there is no Hebrew word in the Bible for human rights. Yet the Bible is the supreme "religious" expression for hundreds of millions of human beings in that it testifies to a millennial-old search for an order of meaning beyond the ordinary events of daily life. In an analogous way, human rights, in its deepest spiritual and philosophic sense, is a central preoccupation of the Biblical literature and tradition, despite the absence of a technical term or category for this fundamental value-concept. Our modern understanding of human rights is decisively shaped by the two central events of Biblical history: the Exodus from Egypt, the covenant at Sinai.

Contrary to the trivialization that has taken place at the hands of Hollywood spectaculars, and even of Sunday school Bible storytelling, the Exodus experience was an epochal event in the history of ideas. It constituted a radical transformation in consciousness in the history of mankind. It altered decisively humankind's orientation toward God, man, society, history—and human rights.

The full significance of that transformation can be understood only when seen against the background of ancient Near Eastern religions and cultures. As the late Professor Ernest Speiser has documented in his essay, "Between Mesopotamia and Egypt,"[*] Biblical monotheism was a divine breakthrough in the mentality of the ancient world, which was dominated by cults and belief systems that were idolatrous, polytheistic, and animal-worshiping. The Pharaoh of ancient Egypt, Speiser reminds us, was a divine

---

[*] Professor Speiser's essay is to be found in an excellent collection of essays by major Jewish scholars called *Jewish Expression*, ed. Judah Goldin (New York: Bantam Books, 1970).

emperor who was regarded as the source of all law, never its servant. Human beings, as epitomized by the slaves of Israel, were treated as chattel, work commodities whose lives could be extinguished by the flick of the royal finger.

The Exodus event was a decisive break with that antihuman mentality. The Lord God of Abraham, Isaac, and Jacob entered into history and brought about the redemption of a slave people. That redemption was two-fold: It involved a spiritual liberation from the darkness of idolatry, primitive superstition, and paganism. It also resulted in redemption from physical oppression and persecution. That double meaning is expressed in the Hebrew word for the Exodus, *Yetziah*, which means both "to go forth" and "to go free."

But the Exodus was not an end in itself. Rather it was a prelude to Sinai. After forty years of trials, temptations, sufferings, and spiritual preparation, the children of Israel were brought to Mount Sinai. Through the gracious initiative and love of God for the children of Israel, he summoned them to enter into a *B'rit*, an everlasting covenant, through which they were to become "a kingdom of priests and an holy nation" (Exod. 19:6).

What an extraordinary divine-human scenario! The Lord God of history, the Lord of all the nations (Jer. 31), out of his free and boundless grace and love, elects a "slave people" to be his "chosen nation" and takes the side of these "untouchable" brick-making slaves in opposition to the imperial power of Pharaoh. Thus, as reenacted by the Jewish people through the annual Passover family seder across the past 3½ millennia until this day, the responsibility to struggle against the injustices suffered by oppressed people everywhere has become a focal attribute of the *imitatio dei*, the living of one's life in accordance with the divine attributes. Simply put, to take seriously the Exodus event means that one cannot be a "religious" or "pious, God-fearing" person and at the same time remain indifferent to human suffering, persecution, prejudice, and injustice.

The Sinai event registered in human consciousness another powerful conviction. Prior to Sinai, the Israelites were perceived as outcasts, a pariah people. In the Egyptian caste system, the lives of the children of Israel were absolutely expendable and were totally subject to the capricious interests of the tyrannical state. The theophany at Sinai ushered in a revolution in human values. By committing their fate and destiny to the covenant with the Lord of Israel, by accepting willingly the call to become the bearers of the Ten Commandments among the family of nations, the slaves of Egypt were transfigured into a state of holiness. "And ye shall be unto Me a kingdom of priests and an holy nation."

Under the divine aspect, slaves who yesterday were considered objects of exploitation for political or economic purposes suddenly became conscious of the infinite preciousness and ultimate worth of human life, its utter sanctity. Created in the image of God, stamped with the dignity that is appropriate to a messianic people charged with the task of advancing redemption in society until the coming of the kingdom at the end of history, no individual human being nor any group of people could ever be allowed again to suffer dehumanization without realizing that an assault against any human personality is nothing other than an assault against the Divine Presence, the *Shechinah*.

To assure that these singular and supremely important lessons of the Exodus and of Sinai did not become merely "memoriams" of past events, nor frozen in the amber of doctrinal or theological propositions without consequence for the actual life of the people, the Israelites were divinely instructed to build a model society in the Promised Land (Canaan, then Palestine, then Israel), in which these human and spiritual values of justice, righteousness, equality, caring, and compassion would become the daily experience of the people of God. Shortly after they had settled in the Holy Land, the Israelites, led by their moral exemplar and lawgiver Moses, established the institutions of the Sabbatical year and the Jubilee year.

Through these pioneering social structures, four fundamental "human rights" were assured to every man, woman, and child in the first Hebrew commonwealth.* In cycles of seven years, cli-

---

* See my essay, "Holy Year 1975 and Its Origins in the Jewish Jubilee Year," in *Jubilaeum* (Vatican City: Vatican Commission for the Holy Year, 1975). Published in English, French, Italian, German, and Spanish.

maxed by the forty-ninth year of the Jubilee (Lev. 25), four categories of spiritual and human liberation were sought for among the
people of Israel:

*Human liberation.* All Hebrew slaves were set free on the basis
of the Lord's teaching, "For unto Me are the children of Israel
slaves; unto Me, and not unto others." The liberty and dignity of
every human being, including slaves, were thereby institutionalized
as basic religious and societal principles.

*Economic liberation.* All property was returned to the original
owners in order to assure economic justice. "The earth is the
Lord's," and therefore human beings are entitled only to the use of
its produce. By establishing the institution of *shmitat karkaot*,
literally, "letting go of the land," no one was allowed to accumulate an overabundance of property while others were condemned
to indentured poverty forever. The Jubilee year was intended to
provide a new opportunity for children of the poor to break out of
the cycle of poverty and to start life with renewed hope and dignity.

*Ecological liberation.* Both in the seventh and in the forty-ninth
years, the land was to lie fallow. Nature was not to be raped by
human greed and lust for wealth. Respect for nature required a
breathing time during which the soil could be restored to its normal vitality. Out of such respect for creation would develop a
restored harmony between human beings and nature. In addition,
Leviticus records, all fruits and vegetables that "grew of themselves," wild growth, were to be made available to everyone who
was hungry—Hebrew citizen, resident alien, the sojourner, the
stranger.

*Educational liberation.* During the Sabbatical and Jubilee years,
the entire people—men, women, and children—were to be instructed in the teachings of the Torah, God's Word for his people.
The revelation was not to become a *gnosis*, esoteric wisdom
preserved solely for the priestly elite, because all Israel was destined to be "a kingdom of priests and an holy nation." The
Sabbatical and Jubilee years thus became one of the first experiments in universal education, with Israel determined to become a
"spiritual democracy."

As we contemplate two centuries of American liberty, it is both fascinating and instructive to reflect on the formative influences that these biblical ideals, values, and institutions had on the shaping of the democratic ethos of the American way of life. Mediated by the Puritans in New England, the Hebrew Scriptures became in many ways the intellectual arsenal of the American Revolution. In the Hebrew Scriptures, the patriots found precedent and inspiration, and the pulpits of the land, where public opinion was molded, resounded with their revolutionary summonses.*

The Exodus from Egypt was the classic model of liberation from tyranny; the colonies of America should also make their exodus. The ten tribes of Israel defied the arrogant son of Solomon and established their own government; the thirteen colonies should do likewise. The Hebrew prophets denounced kings and potentates, and God-fearing Americans may do the same. The call engraved on the Liberty Bell—"Proclaim liberty throughout the land unto all the inhabitants thereof"—selected from the book of Leviticus, was symbolic of the attachment of the Founding Fathers to the Hebrew Scriptures. Revolutionary doctrine became crystallized in the slogan Rebellion to Tyrants Is Obedience to God. Indeed, those were the words which Franklin, Jefferson, and Adams proposed for the seal of the United States; they were to be inscribed around a picture of the children of Israel crossing the Red Sea.

No less potent was the influence of the Hebrew Scriptures in determining the basic political system of the new society that emerged from the War of Independence. To discredit the monarchy, preachers like the bold and brilliant Jonathan Mayhew of Boston held up the warning of the prophet Samuel against royalty. Samuel Langdon, the president of Harvard, considered the Jewish government "a perfect republic," and Ezra Stiles, the president of Yale, found in the American government the fulfillment of biblical prophecy. In his classic work, *History of the Rise and Influence of the Spirit of Rationalism in Europe*, the eminent nineteenth

---

* As Rufus Learsi asserts in his volume on *The Jews in America* (New York: World Publishing Co., 1954).

century historian, William Edward Lecky, declares that "the Hebraic mortar cemented the foundations of American democracy."

There is a real temptation, if not a dangerous tendency, to let observance of the nation's birthday become an escape into the past, a "trip" into nostalgia, and an orgy of national self-congratulation. Nothing could be more alien to all that is best in the biblical and American spirit. Just as the Passover has become an annual event among Jews, not only for the reenactment of the experience of past oppression but especially for vital recommitment to the struggle to overcome persecution and injustice in the present, so annual reflection on whence we have come as a nation ought to afford opportunity for helping to build a better and more just future for the American people and for the whole human family.

In an age of widespread hunger and poverty that exist side by side with overconsumption, at a time when violence, terrorism, and nuclear arms proliferate, when religious-ethnic conflicts pockmark every continent of the inhabited globe, what better starting points are there for rekindling devotion to the cause of human rights, to the sanctity of every human life, and to universal social justice than those of the Exodus and Sinai?